Testing Object-Oriented Software

Life Cycle Solutions

Springer

New York
Berlin
Heidelberg
Barcelona
Hong Kong
London
Milan
Paris
Singapore
Tokyo

Imran Bashir
Amrit L. Goel

Testing Object-Oriented Software

Life Cycle Solutions

 Springer

Imran Bashir
Springfield, VA 22152
USA
imran.bashir@qwest.com

Amrit L. Goel
Dept. of Electrical Engineering/Computer Science
Syracuse University
Syracuse, NY 13244
USA

Library of Congress Cataloging-in-Publication Data
Bashir, Imran.
    Testing object-oriented software : life cycle solutions / Imran
Bashir, Amrit L. Goel.
        p.   cm.
    Includes bibliographical references and index.
    ISBN 0-387-98896-3 (alk. paper)
    1. Computer software—Testing.   2. Object-oriented programming
(Computer science)   I. Goel, Amrit L.   II. Title.
QA76.76.T48B37   2000
005.1′4—dc21   99-16553

Printed on acid-free paper.

Production managed by A. Orrantia; manufacturing supervised by Joe Quatela.
Photocomposed copy prepared from the authors' LaTeX file.
Printed and bound by Maple-Vail Book Manufacturing Group, York, PA.
Cover photo: CORBIS/D. Boone.
Printed in the United States of America.

9 8 7 6 5 4 3 2 1

ISBN 0-387-98896-3 Springer-Verlag New York Berlin Heidelberg   SPIN 10735916

Dedicated
to
my parents (Noor Jehan and Mohammad Bashir)
my children (Danish and Daniyal)
and my wife (Amina)
- I.B.

Dedicated
to
my parents (Shanti Devi and Gujjar Mal)
my children (Alok, Nandita and Neha)
and my wife (Norma)
- A.L.G.

Foreword

The rise of object-oriented (OO) software development seems to have helped improve software quality, but it has not, of course, eliminated all possibility of error. Thus, software testing is at least as important today as it ever has been. Testing, as a centerpiece of quality assurance efforts, only increases in value as society becomes more and more reliant on software.

Testing OO components and even OO systems is not very difficult once you know how to do it. But until now there have been few accounts of how to do it well and none that adequately characterize testing across the life cycle of large OO software production efforts. This book combines insights from research on OO testing with insights from industrial testing efforts to produce an account that should be valuable to anyone interested in the theory and practice of testing OO software.

This book provides extensive coverage of testing methods applicable to OO software development, as well as discussions of underlying concepts and technical underpinnings that enable you to devise additional techniques of your own. It is unlikely that you will apply every test, process, review criterion, or metric described in this book to your software project. If you have a small project, it is unlikely that you will apply more than a few of them. But the breadth of coverage allows you to select and customize them with full knowledge of the alternatives and of the options available if you need to extend testing efforts.

While most of the language-based discussions are based on C++, it is not at all difficult to apply these ideas to other OO programming languages, in particular Java. There are significant differences across these languages, which lead to differences in the nature and prevalence of certain kinds of errors (for example those surrounding memory management). However, most techniques for discovering and dealing with these errors are identical across the two languages.

On a personal note, it is a pleasure to see an ex-student, Imran Bashir (along with Amrit Goel), produce such a useful text. And it is even a pleasure to see code I once helped write undergo such scrutiny in some of the running examples.

Douglas Lea
Professor, State University of New York
Oswego, New York

Preface

Object orientation in software engineering matured from a novelty to a well-established discipline over a span of only few years. While it has not been a silver bullet, object orientation has genuinely changed the way we think about developing software. Today, almost any major software system has at least some influence of object orientation in its development. In the late 1980s object-oriented (OO) technology was utilized for small- to medium-size projects. As confidence of software engineering community grew, OO technology was applied to larger projects. To meet the demands of developing large software systems, impressive advances were made in OO development models, analysis and design techniques, and programming languages. We watched the evolution of the Unified Modeling Language (UML) put an end to "methods war" that had begun in the earlier days of OO technology. We are bearing witness to the explosive growth of the utilization of programming languages like C++ and Java. In spite of this notable maturity of OO in such a short time, testing of OO software has not kept up with the rest of the areas of object-oriented software development. While it is a highly complex and time-consuming life cycle activity, we the software engineering community seems to have neglected object-oriented testing.

Some researchers realized this lack of attention to testing in the object-oriented world and focused their energies to the subject. The first and most obvious candidate for their attention was testing of classes. If we look back, then we note that most of the research activities have been expended on unit testing, or testing of classes; the significance of testing other artifacts of the object-oriented software engineering life cycle have largely been ignored, inadvertently we hope.

This book attempts to provide guidance in object-oriented software engineering life cycle testing issues. This book can be considered a book of testing recipes for the various stages of object-oriented software development. We attempt to cover all major phases of an object-oriented software engineering life cycle. We identify various artifacts at each stage and attempt to provide guidelines for testing these artifacts. The tone of our writing style is informal, concise, and precise. Pragmatically speaking, one may not be able to utilize or need all recipes in this book. Instead, depending on the need, the size of the project, and the availability of tools, these recipes can be utilized, ignored, or customized. We attempt to describe our views in a readily understandable fashion where ever we can. At times, we indulge in details, as one can see in the unit testing of classes. But we deemed it necessary, and we provide examples for ease of comprehension.

In our view, testing should commence with the conception of a project and should continue throughout its life cycle. Hence, we explicitly and individually address testing issues during requirements, design, coding, integration, and system testing phases. We discuss each of these aspects in a template style. Our template consists of the following issues:

- objective
- approach
- activities
- resources
- effort
- acceptance criteria

For each phase of the object-oriented software engineering life cycle, we attempt to provide testing recipes based on this template. While we attempt to provide what we believe to be the most relevant approaches, yet we are aware that we may not have provided all possible approaches.

This book is organized around the major phases of object-oriented software engineering life cycle. The artifacts of each phase are identified in the context of an object-oriented project. Various recipes for testing each of these artifacts are then provided. Depending on reader's role in a project, one or more chapters can be either read or ignored. If this book helps improve the quality of even one software project, we will consider that all our hard work in the wee hours of mornings paid off.

Acknowledgments

From Both of us:

Together, we thank all the staff at Springer Verlag who contributed toward the production of this book. Special thanks go out to Executive Editors, Wayne Yuhasz, John Kimmel, and Bill Sanders. We are greatly indebted to Tony Orrantia for his tremendous help and patience in the production work, and to Fred Bartlett for his help in LATEXfiles. The quality of this book has been greatly improved by the meticulous copy editing work by Penelope Hull.

From Imran Bashir:

Praise be to Allah, Most Gracious, Most Merciful. I would like to thank Allah for commanding me to learn, and for blessing me the opportunities to learn. I would also like to thank many people who have helped me in writing this book - often without knowing it. I would like to thank all my teachers throughout my academics. Doug Lea and Gary Craig introduced to me to object-oriented technology. Gary's comments significantly improved my Ph.D. thesis; some of the chapters in this book are direct outcome of that work. Doug's comments are always a source of encouragement and continuous improvement. Many of his ideas have found way in the following pages. Prof. Goel showed faith in me when I seemed to have lost it. His guidance and friendship is a precious treasure to me. Aref Erfani encouraged me to start writing this book. Parvin Mansouri provided the necessary environment to exercise many of these ideas during a project at LCI International. Rick Sunderman and David Sayre gave me enough liberty to continue working on this book, while I was working on other projects at Qwest Communications.

On a personal note, endless thanks go out to my parents, Noor Jehan and Mohammad Bashir, for their sacrifices, prayers, and support, and for being my greatest teachers. I am greatly indebted to my brother, Dr. Naghman Bashir, who has always stood by me. Special thanks to my sisters, Kanwal Bashir and Iram Bashir, whose love and support has always carried me through good and bad times. Finally, very special thanks to my wife and best friend, Amina Imran, and my sons, Danish Bashir and Daniyal Bashir for their love and patience during the long hours of work and absence necessary to make this book a reality. They have sacrificed a lot of plain family life for the completion of this work. I am endlessly indebted to all of them.

From Amrit Goel:

This book is an outgrowth of Imran Bashir's dissertation. He did a lion share of the work and I thank him for being so selfless and dedicated to finishing the book. Many research projects helped shape my ideas about software engineering for which I extend my appreciation to the funding agencies. Over the course of many years I have enjoyed great professional and personal support from my friends Ray Paul and Jack McKissick for which I an grateful to them. I am also thankful to my Ph.D. students who taught me a lot of what I know. In particular, I am truly grateful to my recent graduate Miyoung Shin for her selfless support during these years. My parents Gujjar Mal and Shanti Devi and my late grandmother Mela Devi sacrificed so much for us to get an education, for which I am eternally grateful. I am deeply obliged to my brothers Anand and Deepak and my sisters Kusum, Arun, Sushma and Suman for their perpetual support and prayers. My children Alok, Nandita and Neha rarely saw me during this academic voyage and neither did the girl I fell in love with, my wife Norma. No words can describe their commitment to me and my love for them.

It has indeed been a long journey from the dirt roads of northern India to some of the most sacred halls of learning that I have been fortunate to even sit in. With a bowed head I say my prayers and thank the almighty God for everything we have been blessed with.

As always any omissions, errors, inaccuracies, and all those good things can be attributed to us. Comments, complaints, and compliments are equally welcome. Electronic mail can be sent to imran.bashir@qwest.com or to goel@cat.syr.edu.

Imran Bashir
Amrit L. Goel

Contents

List of Figures

1
Introduction

There has been a phenomenal growth in the utilization of *object-oriented* technology for developing software systems during this decade. Object-oriented methods have proliferated in software applications for such diverse fields as artificial intelligence, graphics, exploratory programming, physics, telecommunication, banking, stock market, manufacturing, and the internet. As a matter of fact, it is hard these days to name a field that does not utilize the benefits of this technology. Most of the internet applications and applets have been devised using object-oriented design techniques. In fact, object-oriented technology is everywhere and is the single most common factor in software applications being developed at the turn of the millennium.

The term *object-oriented* is used differently by different people. However, they all agree on its promising features for improving the quality of a software system. The popularity of object-oriented philosophy has been due to its claimed support for data abstraction, information hiding, extensional programming, and in particular, reusable software[Mey87]. A major merit of object-oriented programming is its flexibility which allows a software designer to produce reusable, instanciable, information-hiding modules, also known as `classes`[HMF92][SR92]. Due to its widespread acclamation, several research activities have concentrated on the development of object-oriented analysis and design techniques [Boo94][DLF93][JCJO92]. Some authors have also explored the effect of the object object-oriented development techniques on the overall software development process[Doo93]. As a result, a myriad of libraries of classes are publicly and commercially available. These libraries of reusable software components, or classes, are expected to reduce the cost of producing software[Bas93].

To ensure high quality of the software developed from these libraries, it is necessary to ensure that these reusable components are error-free, or at least as error-free as technically possible. Contrary to the conventional wisdom, however, the high quality of these reusable software parts does not guarantee high quality of software as a whole. A software system has many artifacts, including the code written in a programming language, and each of these artifacts can be a source of defects in the software. Hence all aspects and artifacts of software systems must be analyzed for high quality.

Two broad categories of techniques for assuring high-quality software are *formal verification* and *testing*[BG93][Heg89]. Although formal verification is based on a sounder theoretical foundation than testing, it is generally considered impractical for large software products. Therefore program testing has been the most commonly used technique for ensuring software quality.

This book is about testing. It deals not only with the code but also with the other object-oriented software artifacts that are necessary for developing a successful application. This testing is a life cycle activity that helps in preventing, detecting, and removing bugs at each stage and from each artifact of a software system. Because the object-oriented software engineering life cycle and its artifacts are different than traditional software development practices, new testing techniques are mandated. We propose and provide such testing techniques and approaches to address the challenges presented by object-oriented software engineering.

1.1   Why a Book on Testing Object-Oriented Software?

The object-oriented software development process is different than its procedural counterpart. It is neither strictly top-down nor strictly bottom-up. It promotes an iterative and recursive development life cycle[Boo96]. Most authors concur that adoption of object-objected technology impacts every aspect of the software development process as well as everything in software engineering organization[Ber92a]. Almost all the books on various aspects of object-oriented software engineering concur that testing of object-oriented software requires major enhancements to the process of software testing[Pre97]. Yet it is interesting to note that very few authors have gone into the details of the impact of object-oriented software on testing.

Although testing of object-oriented software was addressed as early as 1989[Fie89], serious efforts have proliferated only over the last few years[Bas93][Ove94a][Mar95] [GKH$^+$95][Bin96i][CMLK96a]. Most of these research efforts deal with a single dimension of object-oriented software testing. Many of them deal only with *unit* testing, and a few also address integration testing aspects[Ove94a]. Furthermore, very little effort has been spent on testing as a life cycle issue as compared to other aspects of object-oriented software development. Major object-oriented testing efforts, especially on testing of object-oriented code, have been expended as a point solution in the software life cycle. We strongly believe in testing as an interwoven effort within software engineering. We contend that testing should commence as soon as a software idea is conceptualized. This book provides complete testing solutions for all phases of the object-oriented software engineering life cycle. Testing should run concurrent with the software engineering activities and should not be squeezed into a single phase of the development cycle. A major thrust of this book is testing every tangible item in the development phase of the object-oriented software life cycle.

1.2   Outline of Book

This book is about the testing of object-oriented software. It talks about various aspects of object-oriented software techniques with respect to their impact on testing. First it argues that the testing of object-oriented software should not restricted to a single phase if software engineering; instead it should run concurrently with other development activities. It then describes how testing should be integrated with other phases of software engineering. A class is a basic *unit* of composition for object-oriented software systems. It is the most natural candidate for the definition of a unit in such systems. Therefore, two book chapters are devoted to testing C++ classes. C++ is used as the language of choice for two major reasons. First C++ is the most popular object-oriented language, and second, a large number of commercial and public domain tools are available for C++.

This book is intended for four types of audience.

1. **Software practitioners** who have been using object-oriented technology, and are wondering whether they should change their testing practices and procedures. If an organization has preestablished testing standards and practices, they are most likely geared towards procedural software. This book provides guidance for changing the testing culture for an object-oriented software system.

2. **Managers** who are new to object-oriented software. If an organization is adhering to traditional software development processes while trying to embrace object-oriented technology, it is likely to fail if the development and testing processes and procedures are not adjusted accordingly. For these managers, this book provides an alternate view on the processes and procedures for object-oriented development testing. It not only gives a perspective on testing object-oriented code, but also provides a complete testing solution for all phases of life cycle.

3. **Researchers** who are strictly interested in the development code level unit and integration testing of object-oriented software. This book provides novel ways to test base classes and derived classes. It also proposes a new integration testing technique for collaborating objects.
4. **Students** of object-oriented technology who want to learn about the impact of testing throughout the object-oriented software engineering life cycle.

The book is divided into eleven chapters. Each chapter deals with a single major testing activity in the object-oriented software engineering life cycle. Following the introductory chapter, Chapter 2 talks about software testing, software engineering models, and our proposed software testing model. The impacts of object orientation on testing are detailed in Chapter 3. Chapters 7 and 8 describe unit testing of derived classes and testing of C++ special features, respectively. Chapters 4 through 6 and Chapters 9 through 11 deal with each of the phases in the software engineering life cycle. Each chapter here is divided into six main sections:

- **objective** of the testing phase
- **approach(es)** used during the phase
- testing **technique(s)** employed for the phase
- ordered set of **activities** during the phase
- required **resources** during the phase
- planned **effort** for the phase
- **acceptance criteria** to move to the next development phase

2
Software Process and Testing Models

Software development is, both physically and mentally, an exhausting process. Schedule pressures, lack of resources, inadequate tools, unanticipated server and network down times, and so on are some of the very familiar scenarios. Through all these bumps and jolts emerges a victorious team with a software system that, for the most part, works.

The software life cycle is a story full of compromises. These compromises are achieved either to deliver the software system in a timely manner or to satisfy one set of requirements over the cost of another. Most of these compromises pop up in the form of software bugs during the maintenance phase of a software system. Analysts can make wrong assumptions. Requirements can be misinterpreted by designers. A design can be inconsistent. Developers can make mistakes in coding. The testing phase can be squeezed to make up for the delay in other phases. Development and management teams can have different perspectives on testing, and that can affect the testing process. All of these factors and many more are sources of software bugs.

Errors, unfortunately, are unavoidable in nontrivial software. These errors could be injected into software during any phase of its development or during its maintenance. Testing is the process of detecting such errors[Bas93]. There are various definitions of software testing. According to the IEEE *Glossary of Software Engineering Terminology*[IEE83], *testing* is

> the process of exercising or evaluating a system or system component by manual or automated means to verify that it satisfies specified

requirements or to identify differences between expected and actual results.

Testing has different meaning to different people. A software engineering team may have a different meaning of testing than its management counterpart. Even among a development team, people have a wide range of views about testing. These views vary from if it compiles, it works to a very formal means of automated testing. Reality lies somewhere in between these two extremes.

There are various misconceptions about testing. For example, some people naively believe that during testing they can find all the errors that were injected while they rushed through the earlier stages of development. This fallacious notion stems from the fact that testing is considered as a series of related activities that occur only after a software system has been completely coded, with the intent to find problems in the code[Mos93]. This notion about testing stems from the infamous waterfall model where testing is confined to a single stage in a software life cycle. This limited approach to testing causes the realization of errors at a very late stage where the cost of fixing the errors is relatively much higher. Testing, in fact, should be a complete life cycle activity that runs concurrent to the development activities.

There are two dimensions to software testing. (1)Testing should run parallel with all other software development activities. The more error-prone activities occur in the early stages of development, so testing should commence with the activities of these earlier phases. (2)Testing is not applicable just to the computer programs. Testing is applied to code walk-throughs and inspection of partial and completed classes and methods, to system documentation, to human factors, to system performance, to system sanity and so on. Hence, testing is not only an error detection mechanism but also a means of error prevention.

Testing is a quality assurance process[Mos93]. Software quality has been defined in many ways, including the absence of errors, conformance to specifications, fitness for use, customer satisfaction, standardization and documentation of procedures, zero defects, lots of features, low development cost, elegant programming, user friendliness, and so on[FFN91][Spu94][Wei92]. Of all its definitions, probably the term *fitness for use* describes software quality the best. This definition includes the aspects of *correctness, robustness, extendibility, reusability,* and *compatibility.* For a detailed discussion of these terms the reader is referred to[Ber88].

Testing, therefore, should be considered a major part of an organization's commitment to software quality. Testing is not just an activity, it is a discipline. It is a combination of activities and processes that yearn software quality. Software quality is defined and controlled via a methodology. The extent to which the software quality is defined and controlled determines the extent to which software testing is defined and controlled[Mos93]. Various models of software development process have been proposed. Each model classifies the extent to which an organization controls its software development process.

Most of the software processes are top-down in nature; they are forced onto the software engineers by the upper management. Quality of a software product and of a software development process should stem from within as well. We therefore prescribe both top-down and bottom-up software development process models. The top-down approach, Capability Maturity Model (CMM), is the the one recommended by Software Engineering Institute (SEI). The bottom-up approach is Watt Humphrey's Personal Software Process (PSP). While CMM provides a controlling framework, PSP provides opportunities for engineers to improve the quality of their daily micro activities. A brief description of these two models is given in section 2.1.

2.1   Software Process Models

The IEEE defines a *process* as "a sequence of steps performed for a given purpose"[ANS91]. Paulk et al.[PCCW93] define a *software process* as "a set of practices, methods, activities and transformations that people use to develop and maintain software and the associated products (e.g., project plans, designs documents, code, test cases, and user manuals)." The maturity of a software organization determines the control it has over its development process. *Software process capability* has been defined as "the range of expected results that can be achieved by following a software process." The extent to which a specific process has been explicitly defined, managed, and measured has been termed *software process maturity*.

Many models of software process maturity have been proposed by various authors[PCCW93][Jon86]. Examples of these models include Capability Maturity Model[PWCC95], Software Productivity Research's Assessment Model[Jon94], Crosby's Quality Management Maturity Grid[Cro79], SPICE[KPG95], ESPRIT Bootstrap[Koc], and Trillium[Trida].

There are two major levels of software process improvement; a *macro* level that is driven by upper management and process staffs, and a *micro* level where the process principals are applied on individual basis. On a *macro* level, one can use CMM as an organization-focused process improvement framework. Although CMM provides the basis of a quality process, it does not guarantee it. Effective personal practices of software engineers must be complemented with a facilitating framework like CMM. The bottom-up approach of PSP, the *micro* level process, helps individual software engineers improve their work to produce quality products. CMM and PSP are mutually supportive, where PSP demonstrates twelve of the eighteen CMM key process areas(KPAs).

2.1.1 Capability Maturity Model (CMM)

In August 1986, the Software Engineering Institute (SEI), with assistance from MITRE Corporation, started building a framework for software organizations to improve their software process[PCCW93]. After many years of research and extensive feedback from government and industrial organizations, the SEI published a fully defined software process maturity model. This model, the Capability Maturity Model(CMM) for software, provides organizations with guidance for measuring software process maturity and establishing process improvement programs. The SEI has defined five levels of software maturity. As an organization matures from one level to another, the software process is better defined. This, in turn, leads to better-quality software. The five levels of software maturity range from an informal, ad hoc process to a very well-defined, controlled, and disciplined process. The level of a certain organization is determined by the set of activities described for each level.

The following classification of five maturity levels highlights the process changes at each of these levels. In the following subsections, we briefly look at each of these levels from a testing standpoint.

Level 1: Initial

Level 1 represents the lowest level of software maturity. The *initial* process is an ad hoc process. There are no planned procedures for software development. Schedules, budgets, and product quality are unpredictable, relying heavily on the individual efforts. The development process used for one project cannot be completely described and hence cannot be used for another project. In other words, the process is very individual oriented and hence the rate of success depends on individual efforts.

Testing at this level of software maturity is hardly distinguishable from debugging, which is a separate process[Mos93]. There are no disciplined testing techniques and procedures. Therefore, testing for this level of software maturity is highly ineffective. This manifests itself in many bugs in the final product.

Level 2: Repeatable

For an organization at this level of software maturity, policies to manage software processes and their implementation are established. Planning and management of new projects result from the experience of similar projects that have been completed before. At this level, basic components of software management control have been established. The software managers track budget, schedule, and software functionality. The problems are dealt with as they arise. Hence, the process is more stable and each new project benefits from the practices of earlier similar projects.

Testing for this level of software process maturity is still not very effective. Testing deliverables are usually discarded at the end of the project and hence the approach and procedures for testing remain with the person actually executing the tests. Even if that person is around for the next such project, he or she may have forgotten the past such experiences. Even if they retain that knowledge, it may not be adequate for the future project.

Level 3: Defined

Organizations at the *Defined* level of software process maturity have standard, stable, and consistent software engineering and software management practices. At this level, a standard process for developing and managing software is documented. There is a group in the organization, e.g., a Software Engineering Process Group (SEPG)[FR90], that is responsible for the organization's software activities. Individual project teams tailor the organization's standard process for their specific needs. The well-defined process includes sound software engineering and management procedures. Since the process is well-defined, it is very easy for management to keep track of the technical progress of all projects.

Testing procedures for a level 3 organization are definitely more well-defined than those at preceding levels. However, effective methods, techniques, and tools that support coding, testing, and implementation are neither mature nor plentiful[Mos93]. Many organizations at level 3 of software maturity are still unaware of the latest software testing methods. Thus their approach to software testing is still restricted to a single stage in the software life cycle, which is inconsistent with the latest software engineering practices and with the one recommended in this book.

Level 4: Managed

Organizations mature to the *managed* level when they begin to employ software metrics for improvement of their software development process. An organization at level 4 sets quantitative quality goals for both software products and processes. Data are collected and analyzed from all the projects in the organization. Processes are instrumented with measurements that establish the quantitative foundation for evaluating the software products and processes. The control over the processes is established by defining acceptable boundaries that all processes must fall under.

Testing at level 4 is well defined and is integrated with other phases of software development. Testing groups are defined and roles and responsibilities of members of these groups are established.

Level 5: Optimizing

Continuous process improvement is the goal for organizations at software maturity level 5. Weaknesses of the development process, including testing, are identified and solutions are found to rectify these problems proactively. New tools and technologies are assessed to propose changes to the development process.

Testing at the optimal level is completely integrated with all the other phases of software development. Software quality is improved not only by detection of errors and correction but also by their prevention.

2.1.2 Personal Software Process (PSP)

The PSP is a new SEI technology that has been shown to inject discipline into individual software development practices while improving productivity and quality of the produced products[FHK+97]. PSP alerts software engineers to the employed processes and their performance. They learn to measure and analyze their work and set new goals and achieve them. PSP has been called "a strategy for professional self-development and enhanced productivity"[Hum96]. Some of the potential benefits of the PSP include reduced code defects, better estimation and planning, enhanced productivity, better understanding of individual skills, and improvement of personal performance[Hum96].

PSP is formally introduced to software engineers in a series of seven progressive steps shown in figure 2.1. Each of these steps includes the elements of the prior steps. The incremental introduction of the practices in each step helps in disciplined engineering of individual software development methods.

Personal Measurement (PSP0)

The first step in PSP is *personal measurement*, labeled as level PSP0. Engineers begin by learning the application of PSP forms and scripts to their personal work. Engineers make two types of personal measurements, *development time* and *defects*(both injected and removed). There are three phases in PSP0: planning, development, and postmortem. PSP0.1 adds a coding standard, size measurement, and the Process Improvement Proposal (PIP) form. The PIP form is utilized to record problems, issues, and ideas for improvement.

PSP0 and PSP0.1 are the self-assessment steps to ascertain where the personal process stands. One has to evaluate the current state of a process to make any improvements to it. PSP0 helps identify and record the present state of affairs for later improvement.

Personal Planning (PSP1)

Once the attributes of a personal process have been measured, planning to improve is introduced at PSP1 and is called *personal planning*. Software engineers use a linear regression-based estimate the sizes and development times for new programs, based on their personal data.

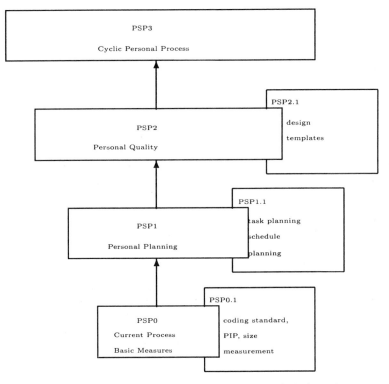

FIGURE 2.1. Personal Software Process (PSP) Evolution.
(adapted from[Hum96])

PSP1.1 adds schedule and task planning. At this level, engineers learn

- the relationship between the sizes of their programs and their associated development time
- how to make achievable commitments
- to plan their work
- to establish a basis for tracking their work

Personal Quality (PSP2)

Defect management is introduced at PSP2, also known as *personal quality.* It has been observed that most software errors are simple typos and/or dumb mistakes[Hum96]. Engineers usually feel that these mistakes can be eradicated through hard work. Unfortunately, things can get worse without proper defect management. PSP2 teaches engineers to construct and use checklists for design and code reviews. They realize the significance of early defect prevention and detection.

Design specification and analysis techniques, along with defect prevention, process analyses, and process benchmarks, are introduced at PSP2.1.

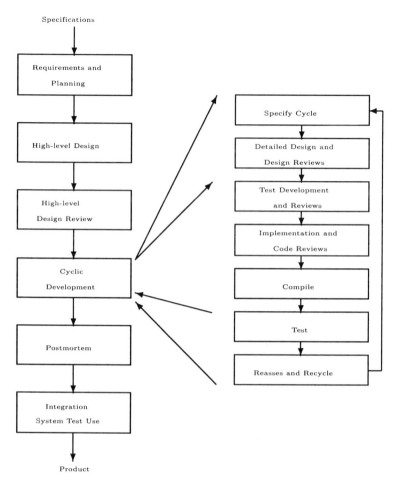

FIGURE 2.2. Cyclic Personal Process (PSP3).

(adapted from[Hum96])

At this level engineers are taught how to address the completion criteria for their work.

Cyclic Personal Process (PSP3)

The final step in PSP is PSP3. It deals with issues involved in developing large-scale problems. The focus is still on individuals, however. The intent is to scale PSP2 up to large-scale software. The general approach is to sub-divide the large-scale problem into PSP2-size pieces, which in turn are designed and developed in an incremental fashion. That is why it is rightfully called a *cyclic personal process*. It is shown in figure 2.2.

PSP3 provides a framework for integrating PSP2-size iterations. Each iteration is a complete PSP2 that includes design, code, compile, and test. Design, test development, and code reviews are included in each PSP2 iteration. This cyclic development approach is very similar to the one proposed by Booch[Boo96].

2.2 Object-Oriented Software Development and Testing Model

Testing is one area in software engineering where the gap between research knowledge and industry practice has been considerably large. There are potentially a number of reasons for this, which depend on what side of the issue the person you are talking to is on. One reason that both sides would agree on is that it requires additional and diligent effort on the part of an organization to have an extensive testing process. This supplemental effort does not have to exist if both development and testing processes can be merged together as an integrated software development process. An important goal of both software development and software testing processes is to deliver quality software that meets or exceeds user expectations. In most organizations, these two processes are implemented independently. This separation of processes results in some redundant and unnecessary effort. Integrating the two provides a better framework for coordination between the individual goals as well as for removal of redundancy between the common goals of the two processes.

2.2.1 Object-Oriented Software Development Model

Booch[Boo96] defines a *successful* project as one whose deliverables satisfy or exceed user expectations, is developed within the estimated time and budget, and is resilient to changes. Based on this definition, he further describes five essential attributes of successful projects:

- ruthless focus on the development of a system
- strong result-oriented culture
- effective use of object-oriented modeling
- strong architectural vision
- well-managed, iterative, and incremental life cycle methodology

Although all these traits are imperative for the success of a project, we want to focus the reader's attention on the last one. A successful project, more often than not, is a result of an iterative and incremental process. An organization not following such a process may, at times, be triumphant in producing a *successful project,* but nothing can be said about the future of that organization or the projects it undertakes.

On the other hand, an organization following a true incremental and iterative process for its projects produces *reliable products*. The process is *iterative* in the sense that the architecture is refined in each iteration by utilizing the experience of previous iteration. The process is *incremental* from the standpoint that the strategic and tactical decisions are refined through each cycle of analysis, design, and evolution [Boo94]. Most of the other popular object-oriented methods promote this iterative and incremental approach. We have taken Booch's development methodology as an example and have tried to integrate the testing framework into it.

Booch describes two constituents of a software development process, a *micro process* and a *macro process*. The *micro* element of software development serves as the framework for the incremental and iterative approach to development. Micro process is closely related to Humphrey's Personal Software Process (PSP)[Hum96] and to Boehm's spiral model[Boe88]. It includes the daily activities in the professional life of a developer or of a small team of developers. Typical activities in a micro process include identification of classes, identification of semantics of classes, identification of class relationships, and specification of class interfaces and implementation. PSP, described in section 2.1.2, supplements the quality control methods like design reviews, test reviews, and code reviews.

The *macro* process, on the other hand, provides the framework for controlling and managing the micro process. The *macro* process is closely related to the traditional waterfall model of software development.

2.2.2 Parallel Testing Model

Software development is an error-prone process. Errors can be injected during every step on the way through various sources. Correction of these errors is less costly in the earlier stages of software development than in later stages. To correct an error, however, it must first be detected. Testing is one way of detecting errors. This argument naturally leads to the philosophy of testing every phase of software development.

Testing at each and every step of the has been reinforced by Hetzel[Het88]. We call concurrent testing *Parallel Testing*. A model of parallel testing is shown in figure 2.3 along with the *macro* software development process described in section 2.2.1.

Similar to the object-oriented software development model, the object-oriented software testing model consists of the *micro* and *macro* processes. The macro process of testing is the controlling framework for the micro process of testing. The micro process, on the other hand, deals with the daily life activities of a tester. While the macro process runs in parallel with the macro process of development, the micro process is in sync with the micro phase of development. The following subsections describe each of the processes in some detail.

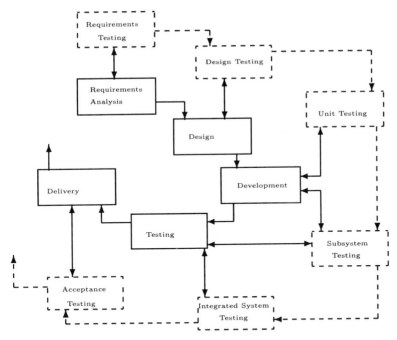

FIGURE 2.3. Parallel Testing Life Cycle for Object-Oriented Software.

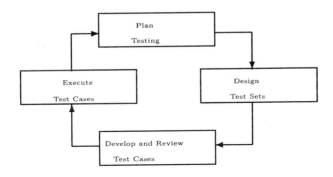

FIGURE 2.4. Micro Process In Object-Oriented Software Testing.

Micro Process of OO Testing

The micro process of object-oriented software testing tends to provide better testing control over the iterative and incremental micro process of object-oriented software development. It reflects the daily activities in the life of a tester. This process repeats itself multiple times in each of the macro phases of software testing. The micro process of testing consists of four major activities, shown in figure 2.4:

Plan the Testing: The objective during this activity is to identify what needs to be tested during this iteration of testing. This planning not only includes the new items to be tested but also any previous items that need to be regression tested.

Design Test Sets: The next activity in the micro process is to design the test sets that provide enough coverage to satisfy the goals set forth for this iteration of testing. Again, this phase includes new test cases as well as any previous test sets that can be reused.

Develop and Review the Test Cases: This activity involves defining test cases under each test set defined in the previous phase. These test cases are then reviewed themselves to ensure that they truly reflect the objective of this iteration of micro testing.

Execute Test Cases: The final stage involves the execution of the test cases. During this stage, any required regression testing is also performed. The results of this stage are then taken into consideration for the next iteration of testing.

Macro Process of OO Testing

At the macro level, there are six stages of parallel testing of object-oriented software, shown in figure 2.3:

Requirements Testing: This phase involves the validation of methods and processes to collect requirements, checking for the completion and consistency among the requirements, and removal of any duplicate requirements. It is performed during the requirements collection and requirements analysis stages. Details of *requirements analysis testing* are given in chapter 4.

Design Testing: The design is tested to ensure that the proposed architecture is correct, consistent, and complete. This phase includes checking for the coverage of all requirements by the design. *Design testing* is detailed in chapter 5.

Unit Testing: The goal of this phase of testing is to ensure that individual pieces, or units that form the system, conform to their specifications and expected behavior. The definition of a unit in an object-oriented system is different from its counterpart in a procedural system. Hence the approaches used to test a unit are different as well. *Unit testing* of object oriented software is discussed at length in chapters 6 and 7.

Subsystem Testing: A subsystem is a set of logically related units. Once units have been verified, they are tested as a collection during this phase of testing. The details of *subsystem testing* are discussed in chapter 10.

Integrated System Testing: The objective of this phase is to test the integrated system for functionality, performance, reliability, and human factors. *Integrated system testing* is discussed in chapter 11.

Acceptance Testing: Once the system is declared ready by the development team, it is tested by an external organization. If the system passes this test, it is considered ready to be shipped out. *Acceptance testing* is discussed in chapter 11.

2.2.3 Testing Ripples

As described earlier, testing is an integral part of software development. Testing at earlier stages usually reduces the number of defects in the later stages of development. In this section, we describe a testing framework that runs concurrent with the development process. This framework can be pictorially described in the form of *ripples*, shown in figure 2.5.

If a small stone is thrown into still water, the water moves outward in ripples with a slight rise and fall. An iterative and incremental model of software testing works the same way. At each macro stage of development, the main focus switches back and forth between the development and testing, the rise and fall effect. Figure 2.5 enhances this ripple effect of software testing with an eight-dimensional matrix. Each axis in the matrix represents a certain aspect of software testing for a given stage. The eight dimensions of this matrix, starting clockwise at 12 o'clock, are as follows:

Testing Phase: This axis identifies the phase of development we are in. The other phases are named from the testing standpoint.

Begin Date: This axis names the date each stage of software testing begins.

End Date: The axis identifies the planned completion date for the respective testing phase.

Environment: This axis identifies what environment would be used for the given testing phase. The environment includes identification of specific machines, their configurations, their physical locations, and so on.

Resources: This axis entails the personnel and other required resources for the given phase of software testing.

Testing Techniques: This axis indicates the software testing techniques that the team plans on using during a certain phase of software testing.

Deliverables: The output, or the deliverables, for a certain phase of software testing are described along this axis. They include any software problem reports, results of test execution, and so on.

Inputs: Along this axis are the inputs required for the associated software testing phase. They may include test cases, test sets, and so on.

We use this software testing framework throughout this book.

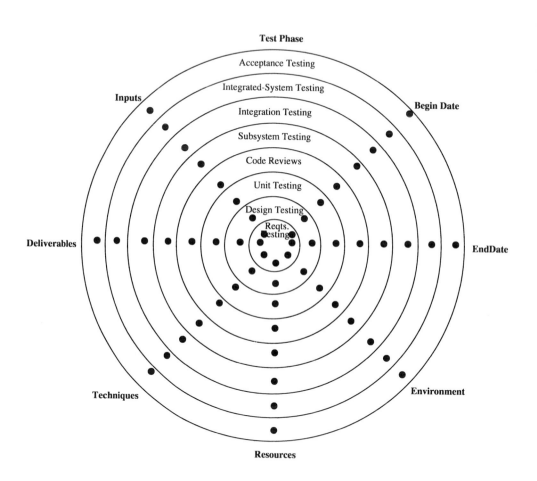

FIGURE 2.5. Software Testing Framework in Software Engineering Life Cycle.

2.3 Summary

Traditionally, software testing has been constrained to a single phase of the software life cycle. Modern software engineering practices offer a model where testing activities run concurrent with the other development undertakings.

Ever-increasing complexity and quality requirements of software systems warrant error identification as early in the software life cycle as possible. Our parallel testing model supports this notion by coordinating the test and development activities. This reduces the system testing load in two ways. (1)It distributes the system testing load throughout the software life cycle; (2)it prevents errors from creeping into the following phases by catching them as they occur.

3
Impact of Object Orientation on Testing

Most current software testing techniques are congruent with functional-based software. A *unit* of software is either tested against its specifications or against some code-coverage criterion to execute its identified paths. Object-oriented software is radically different from its procedural counterpart[Amb96]. Procedural programming relies on procedural autonomy with no interaction through nonlocal variables. Object-oriented programming, in contrast, discourages procedure autonomy and relies on the packaging of procedures that share an object's local variables[CS93]. The roots of object-oriented programming style lie in the *encapsulation* and *abstraction* of abstract data types[Cop92]. Object-oriented technique provides an abstract way of thinking about a problem in terms of problem-domain concepts, rather than in computer concepts [RBP⁺91]. These concepts are eventually converted into computer concepts, but the abstract way of object-oriented thinking provides a completely different implementation compared with the functional, design-based implementation. Object-oriented languages provide many new constructs that aid in the implementation of an object-oriented design. Since these concepts are not prevalent in traditional software, existing software testing techniques fail to suffice for completely testing object oriented software[CMLK96a].

On a similar note, object-oriented techniques impact software standards and procedures. During transition to a new technology, some of the standard practices applicable to old technology are still valid. Some standard practices and procedures, however, have to be modified, while others are totally discarded. Migration of an organization from traditional software development to object-oriented software development greatly impacts its culture. The repercussions of this cultural change on an organization's standards and procedures must be carefully evaluated. Since testing of the software in an organization is also based on the traditional software philosophy, the organization must determine the impact of this technology transition on its testing techniques[Ber92b].

Object orientation is usually employed to improve productivity and efficiency of a software development organization[Hun95b]. Improved productivity implies that the same functionality will be produced in less time. Consequently more effort should be expended on testing since higher-complexity software is being produced in less time. This increased complexity is conducive to more error opportunities in novel ways. Less time spent in producing the code should free up more time for testing the code.

Some of the inherent characteristics of object-oriented technology that distinguish it from its traditional counterpart are *encapsulation, information hiding, inheritance, reuse,* and *abstraction* [Bas93]. These attributes are discussed in detail in sections 3.1 to 3.5, and their impact on the software testing process is also identified. This discussion raises some issues that are fundamental to the testing process and must be considered while testing object-oriented software. Testability of object-oriented systems is also compared in this discussion with its procedural counterparts. Finally, testability of object-oriented systems is briefly discussed in section 3.6.

3.1   Encapsulation

Encapsulation is a tool through which we enclose one or more items within a physical or logical container[Ber92a]. It should be mentioned here that the visibility of the items inside the "capsule" is not part of the encapsulation definition. One of the best definitions of *encapsulation* has been provided by Wirfs-Brock et al.[WBWW90]:

> The concept of *encapsulation* as used in an object-oriented context is not essentially different from its dictionary definition. It still refers to building a capsule, in this case a conceptual barrier, around some collection of things.

There are different levels of encapsulations, which depend on the design approach used for describing a system. Berard[Ber92a] identifies three kinds of encapsulations, *low-level, mid-level,* and *high-level.* The low-level encapsulation includes things like arrays and records. At the mid-level of encapsulation are entities like subprograms and subroutines. At the top level, high-level encapsulation, are things like classes, packages and objects. The biggest impact of encapsulation on the testing of object-oriented software is the change in the definition of a unit.

For object-oriented software, the unit of testing is not a subroutine or a function any more. The conventional approaches to software testing are based on the assumption that the software is developed using the top-down functional approach. So traditionally when testers talk about *unit testing*, the underlying assumption is that a basic unit of testing is a subprogram or a subroutine. With the switch to object-oriented software, one wonders if the basic unit of software testing is still a subprogram. In object-oriented world, the subprograms are usually not stand-alone entities. Instead, subprograms and functions are associated with an object and their behavior depends on the state of the object. An object encapsulates its state and the associated functions. Hence, the most obvious unit of testing is an object, since the software is based on the interaction of these objects. Thus one of the major impacts that object orientation has on software testing is that the basic unit of software testing is an *object* or a `class`.

Berard[Ber92a] identifies two major impacts of encapsulation on testing of object-oriented software. The first one is the change in the definition of a unit, while the second one is the impact of this change on integration testing. Let's see how an object, as a unit of software testing, impacts integration testing.

In integration testing, many tested modules are combined into subsystems incrementally, which are then tested. In procedural programming, the modules to be combined are sub-programs, but now the unit of integration is an object instead. Objects can be combined into *components*, or objects can be *aggregated* to form *composite* objects. An object-oriented software testing technique must consider the impact of this object aggregation and composition. Now the question arises whether objects can be integrated into systems just like subprograms. If not, then what would be the impact of this on overall integration testing strategy? A novel technique for object integration is detailed in chapter 10.

3.2   Information Hiding

Berard[Ber92a] notes a big misconception in the definitions of *encapsulation, information hiding,* and *abstraction.* A whole chapter in his book is devoted to elucidating the differences between these three concepts.

Information hiding, like most of the other concepts in the object-oriented world, has no standard definition. A myriad of definitions have been proposed by different people. For a survey of these definitions, see Berard[Ber92a]. Booch[Boo91] defines information hiding as follows:

> The process of hiding all the details of an object that do not contribute to its essential characteristics; typically, the structure of an object is hidden, as well as the implementation of its methods.

Encapsulation permits, physically or logically, a few items to be bound together. It does not say anything about the visibility of each of these items. Information hiding, on the other hand, permits us to suppress or hide some of the inessential details of an entity.

The advocates of object orientation proclaim *information hiding* as one of the most important characteristics of this philosophy. Despite all its benefits, information hiding may be a strain on the life of a software tester. Information hiding makes part of an object inaccessible to the rest of the world. To test a method, if a tester is checking the state of an object before and after the invocation of the method, then the tester needs to access the internal state of the object. The internal state of the object, however, is hidden from the tester. Although state-reporting methods[1] of an object can be used to inspect the internal state of an object, they raise two new issues. First, an object may not support, as its public interface, state-reporting methods for each of its internal data members. Second, even if an object supports a complete set of state-reporting methods, these methods have not been validated and hence cannot be trusted. There should be some strategy that tests state-reporting methods.

3.3 Abstraction

Abstraction is a technique through which humans cope with complexity [Boo91]. As in the case of information hiding and encapsulation, different people define abstraction differently. Booch has combined some of these viewpoints to give this definition of abstraction [Boo91][Boo94]:

> An abstraction denotes the essential characteristics of an object that distinguish it from all other kinds of objects and thus provide crisply defined conceptual boundaries, relative to the perspective of the viewer.

Abstraction separates the essential behavior of an object from its implementation. It focuses on the outside view of an object. In object-oriented software, we strive to build entity abstractions, [Boo91] which means that we identify objects that represent useful models of problem-domain entities. unit of abstraction in an object-oriented system, an object can be treated as a black box. This black-box view of an object is acceptable from a client's point of view but is not of much use to the tester of the black box, especially while performing its structural testing. The information abstracted by the object is required to satisfactorily test this object. Therefore a testing strategy for object-oriented software should also take this fact of abstraction of information into account.

---

[1] Also known as *inspectors*.

3.4 Inheritance

Barring trivial applications, there are more abstractions in the systems than one can comprehend easily. Encapsulation and information hiding help us manage this complexity by suppressing some inessential details of the system. Sometimes this is not enough. It has been observed that a set of abstractions form a kind of hierarchy in a problem domain[Boo91][Boo94]. Our understanding of the problem is greatly reduced if this hierarchical structure of the abstractions is recognized. Inheritance is one of the most essential tools through which we organize the hierarchical structure of a complex system. Stroustrup[Str91] observes that "a concept does not exist in isolation; it co-exists with related concepts and derives much of its power with relationships with related concepts." Inheritance allows us to represent these relationships between concepts. According to Booch[Boo91],

> inheritance defines a relationship among classes, wherein one class shares the structure or behavior defined in one or more classes.

There are two ways of looking at the inheritance relationship in a system, *essential* inheritance, which implies inheritance of specifications, and *incidental* inheritance, which implies inheritance of implementation [Sak89]. The inheritance of specification provides specialization-generalization hierarchies in the system, whereas the inheritance of implementation is primarily a code-reuse mechanism. Here we look at the impact of inheritance of specification on the testing of object-oriented software. The effects of inheritance of implementation will be looked at when we consider the impacts of reuse on testing.

There are two dimensions to inheritance of specification, *single* inheritance and *multiple* inheritance. If an object acquires characteristics directly from only one object, then it is called *single* inheritance. If the characteristics are acquired directly from more than one object, then it is termed as *multiple* inheritance[Ber92a]. Any strategy for testing object-oriented software has to accommodate the different types of inheritance relationships as specified by the language. For example in C++[ES90], *public* or *private* inheritance imply an "is-a" or a "part-of" relationship, respectively, between the derived class and the base class. So the testing strategy must consider the possibility of substitution of a base class where a derived class has been used and so on.

3.5 Reuse

As stated in section 3.4, the inheritance of implementation implies the inheritance of all or part of the underlying implementation of the base class to the derived class. The derived class reuses the implementation of the part or all of the interface of the base class. This code-reuse is a very tricky issue, depending on the language. In C++[ES90], for example, member functions can be declared *virtual* or *nonvirtual* and depending upon these declarations, methods can be redefined or overridden in the derived class. Depending on the same declarations, the substitution of a pointer to a base class by a pointer to a derived class can invoke different member functions. Mechanisms that can invoke different member functions, depending on the pointer type of the object, must be explicitly considered by the testing strategy.

Another dimension to inheritance and reuse is to determine if a member function that has been tested in a base class needs retesting when it is inherited in the derived class. Testing of a derived class may be affected by the amount of retesting required for each of its base classes. In some cases, the test cases generated for the base class may be used to test a derived class as well. Some of these issues have been addressed by Perry and Kaiser [PK90], Turner[TR92b], and Harrold et al.[HMF92].

3.6 Testability of Object-Oriented Systems

Traditionally, *testability* has been defined as a measure of the ability to select inputs that satisfy certain structural testing criteria[Cor95]. This definition implies that if an input distribution can be selected that completely satisfies a selected code coverage criterion, then the *testability* of the program under test is 100%. Over the last few years, the term *testability* has been redefined by Voas[Cor95], and has been generally accepted, as

a prediction of the probability of software failure occurring due to the existence of a fault.

This new definition implies that software testability is related to the ability of software to hide faults for a selected input distribution.

Generally, the testability of object-oriented systems has been found to be lower than its procedural counterpart[Voa97]. One can attribute the lower testability of object-oriented systems tothe information hiding and abstraction mechanisms. For the most part, an object-oriented system tends to accept more information than it reveals. For example, a method may accept a set of inputs, modify its internal state, and generate a single output. This *internal state collapse*[Cor95] tends not to propagate the faults to the output. Integrated circuit designers call such a phenomenon *observability*, the ability to view the internal state of a node in an embedded circuit[Voa97]. Since the *observability* of a `class` tends to be low, it manifests itself in low *testability*.

Testability of object-oriented systems should be measured and controlled at all levels of software development, requirements testability, design testability, code testability, and test techniques testability. In the following chapters, we provide recommendations and guidelines for increasing the testability at each of these levels.

3.7 Summary

Object-oriented software testing is significantly different from its procedural counterpart. Some of the notable differences are the following.

- The unit of testing for an object-oriented software is an *object* versus a *procedure* as in traditional software. Since there is a fundamental difference between an object and a procedure, it impacts the unit testing strategies.
- The definition of unit also impacts the integration testing strategies.
- Typically the state-representing data members of a class are not accessible by an external object. Since the state of an object is crucial in determining the correct behavior of an object, it impacts the strategies for testing it.
- A class may inherit attributes from another class. During testing of a derived object, both local and inherited attributes must be taken into consideration.
- A derived class may redefine some method of its base class in such a way that the testing of the base class may be necessary.
- Contrary to common perception, an inherited method also needs retesting as a method of derived class.

4
Requirements Testing

Requirements testing has been one of the most neglected areas in the software testing world. Until recent years, the results of requirements collections and requirements analysis were not tested at all. With the advent of modern software engineering techniques, testing these results has become more acceptable, though not widely practiced. Requirements testing is still an ad hoc and informal process. Lack of attention to requirements testing is evident from the scarcity of requirements testing tools.

In this chapter, we discuss testing of an object-oriented software system during the requirements analysis phase of its development. The effect of the object-oriented approach on the collection and analysis of requirements will also be discussed.

One of the foremost issues in the use of object-oriented technology has been the concept of mixing components from a structured development process with those of an object-oriented development process. Various authors have expressed their views on this issue[DLF93] and have denied the viability of these combinations. One of the key problems of combining structured requirements analysis with object-oriented design is the inability to derive generic and other objects from the output of the analysis phase. Hence, we believe that if we adopt object-oriented design and implementation techniques, object-oriented requirements analysis techniques must also be used.

It has been suggested that with the emergence of object-oriented technology, the analysis and design phases are merging with each other. This viewpoint is correct up to a certain extent. There will always be certain objects that are carried unchanged through the different software development phases. However, one cannot overlook the inherent differences between the different phases of software development. Analysis aims at precisely and clearly defining a problem for which the design intends to find a solution. Hence, although the object-oriented technology has created a grey area between the analysis and design phases, the objective and the focus of each phase is well separated.

4.1 Objective

In an object-oriented requirements analysis phase, analysts talk to customers and through various iterations deliver the requirements to the designers. The results of the requirements analysis is a description of the function of the system, along with statements about performance and required resources[DLF93]. These results can be captured through various formal and informal documents whose aim of these documents is to accurately and unambiguously state the known intricate details of a specific problem. Some of the most commonly used tools for capturing and analyzing these requirements follow.

Prototyping: One of the common elements of object-oriented analysis, prototyping plays a crucial role in properly determining the exact parameters of the problem. It also helps customers define what they want and what they do not want in the desired system.

Graphical User Interface: GUI is one element of the delivered system through which a customer interacts with the system. It must be as close to the customer's wishes as possible. Different screen layouts are sketched or prototyped and are shown to the customer for feedback and subsequent improvement.

Requirements Specification Document: All requirements for a desired system are listed in this document. It serves as a contractual agreement between a customer and a development team about the desired properties and behavior of the expected system.

Domain Object Model: The problem domain is captured via a domain object model. Each object in the model refers to either a tangible thing or a mental concept identifiable for the customers of the desired system.

Use Cases: A use case[JCJO92] is a specific way in which the desired system may be used. It outlines the set of ordered events that take place in certain function of the system. Use cases are a very useful tool for capturing the exact behavior of the desired system. Possible use of use cases for object-oriented testing are described in[Maj98].

The objective of requirements testing is to validate each of the outputs of the analysis phase to ensure quality and to eradicate any errors as early in the process as possible. Testing of requirements involves three basic issues. Two of these issues have also been identified by Hetzel[Het88].

1. **Correctness** of requirements is a fundamental assumption for designers. Pragmatically speaking, requirements keep evolving, and they must clearly state the customers' true wishes. Ambiguity of the natural language is a source of many misconceptions about software requirements. Analysts must ensure that the vague words in requirements statements are replaced. Since requirements are the first step in the software engineering process, the statements must be correct because they become the foundation for all the software engineering activities that follow[Pre97].

2. **Completeness** of requirements implies that the problem must be completely and clearly specified. Requirements include *functional, performance, resource* and *quality,* requirements. Functional requirements detail the black-box view of the system. They specify the desired behavior of the system under specified input conditions. Performance requirements outline the response times of the system for various functionalities. Resource requirements refer to the resources available for the execution of the desired system[DLF93]. Quality requirements include the reliability and robustness of the system under specified conditions.

3. **Consistency** of a set of requirements is another major aspect of its testing. It is very common for users to outline contradictory requirements for a system. These incongruent requirements must be caught and eliminated during requirements testing. Similarly, users may have given redundant requirements. Redundant requirements can often be a source of errors since although two redundant requirements may mean the same functionality, they may be interpreted differently by different designers or implementors.

4.2 Approach

Theoretically, *requirements testing* is a prudent concept with high potential payoffs. In practice, unfortunately, it is given little to no attention. Schedule pressures, lack of software engineering standards and procedures, lack of insight into the benefits of requirements testing, and the haste to get to the coding stage are some of the common implicit reasons for neglecting requirements testing. Lack of attention to requirements testing has resulted in a dearth of necessary tools.

Collection and analysis of requirements for a system is not a trivial task. Since there are almost no formal tools available, the requirements are usually captured in the English language. English is ambiguous by its very nature. A very well-stated requirement may be interpreted differently by different people. A single misinterpreted requirement may be the source of myriad errors in the code and in the functionality of the system.

The general approach for testing the output of the requirements collection and analysis phase is gathering feedback from the end-users and
reviewing it with the rest of the development team. Feedback from the
users addresses the first major issue in requirements testing. This feedback
helps in filling the holes in the requirements documents. Analysts, however,
are responsible for guiding the users in identifying the key elements of the
requirements documents. The feedback is obtained through validating the
use cases, validating the requirements specifications document, and showing the users the prototypes. A domain object model is created to capture
the problem domain in a more formal manner. Walk-throughs with the development team improve the domain object model by eliminating incorrect
relationships between classes and their stated behavior.

4.3 Activities

Four major outputs of the requirements analysis phase are the requirements
specifications, use cases, the domain object model, and the prototypes.
Figure 4.1 outlines the activities involved in requirements testing.

Requirements are tested in an incremental manner. Analysts must decide the order in which to test requirements based on system functionality,
subsystem delineation, or any other decomposition technique. As new
requirements emerge, they are accommodated into the requirements specifi-

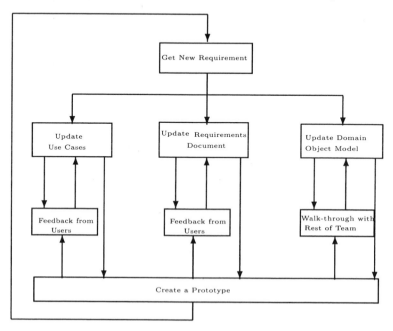

FIGURE 4.1. Object-Oriented Requirements Testing Activities

cations document, into use cases, and into the domain object model. These documents are then internally reviewed with the rest of the team. Based on the internal review feedback, the documents are modified. Once the whole team agrees on the consistency and accuracy of the documents, they are taken to the users for their review. Novice analysts will be surprised at how quickly the users can change their mind of course unintentionally about a certain functionality of the system. Feedback from the users leads to additional changes in each document. These changes are reviewed in other iterations of the internal and external reviews until everyone concurs on the given set of requirements. This set of requirements may then be prototyped by the team to get better insight into the accuracy and consistency of the requirements. The results are taken to the users again for eliminating any inconsistent or ambiguous requirements. Requirements may then be added to the system and to the prototype for the next iteration of cycle.

A tool that has worked very well for some of the projects that we have worked on is a requirements testing matrix (RTM). An RTM lists each of the requirements of the desired system along with the use cases and test cases that cover the requirement. A typical RTM is given in table 4.1.

As requirements are collected, they are added to the *requirement* column. Use cases number that cover each requirement are entered into the second column. The third column lists the test cases that verify the requirement, the fourth column identifies the prototype in which that requirement was prototyped, and the fifth column identifies whether or not the requirement has been validated with the user.

4.3.1   Typical Activities in Requirements Testing

Three possible means of testing software requirements are testing through understanding the requirement, testing through test-case design, and testing through prototypes[Het88]. The following typical set of activities uses all three means of testing the requirements. This order of the activities is not graven in stone however. The activities should be considered a general framework and be adapted to suit individual needs and projects.

1. **Select Requirement:** Select one requirement or a subset of requirements from the requirements testing matrix. Selecting the requirement

Requirement	Use Cases	Test Cases	Included in Prototype Version	Validated with User?

TABLE 4.1. Typical Requirements Testing Matrix (RTM).

for testing can be a hard problem by itself. One possible solution to this problem is to first classify the requirements by functionality. Then order the requirements by simplicity and/or ease of understanding. Finally, order the requirements of the functionality, again simple requirements listed before the complex ones. Choose the first requirement for the functionality for testing.

2. **Comprehend Requirement:** Understand the requirement in terms of what the user wishes to get out of the system. Clearly understanding a requirement is the key to testing it. Although a requirement may look very simple and precise, it is a good idea to discuss your interpretation of the requirement with the user or with the person who gathered the requirement.

3. **Mentally Test Requirement:** Ask yourself how the system will be used to test this requirement. A requirement may be clear, but more insights about a requirement can be achieved by asking oneself how a system can be tested for the given requirement.

4. **Update Use Case:** Create or update a use case that would cover system usage for this requirement. Use cases are a very useful tool for clearly specifying the interaction of the user with the desired system. Outlining the behavior of the user and of the system in a series of well-defined steps ensures that both user and analyst understand the desired behavior of the system. It also helps the user to think clearly about haves and have-nots of the desired system. These use cases can later serve as the basis for developing test cases. Each use case is assigned a meaningful name/number. The list of use case(s) is then documented against the requirement under test in the RTM.

5. **Create Test Case:** Create a test case that would satisfy this requirement. Developing a test case to determine the conformance of a system to a certain requirement gives a better insight into the requirement. Test cases can then be assigned numbers and documented in the RTM. These test cases are later used for integrated system testing and for acceptance testing.

6. **Test Completeness:** Check for the completeness of the requirement by asking what the system would do under similar conditions under different input values and so on. The requirement may be incomplete in terms of defining the response of the system under certain input conditions. Testers should ask and answer these questions to complete the specifications of the system for the given functionality.

7. **Test Consistency:** Check for the consistency of the requirements by comparing each requirement against the list of other already-tested requirements. First check against the requirements of the same functionality. If no inconsistencies are found, then check against the requirements of the rest of the functionalities of the system. In case of any inconsistency, check with users to remove the inconsistent requirement(s).

8. **Prototype:** Create or update a prototype to see how that rec is satisfied by the system. Every requirement may look consiste and testable to both analysts and the users. Prototypes are cı determine the feasibility of the requirement in terms of implemı within the schedule of the project. One typical example of prototypes is the graphical user interface. On paper, users may have listed certain data on a screen. Prototyping and showing that screen to the users often changes their mind about how detailed they want the screen to be.

9. **Solicit Feedback:** Show the prototype to the users to get their feedback. Reviews by the users are the biggest testing tools the analysts have at hand. This tool is not as frequently used as it ought to be, which leaves big misunderstandings between what the users want and what the development team is building. Just remember, no matter what state-of-the-art technology or software engineering practice is employed, if a system does not meet the specifications as perceived by the users, it is going to end up in a virtual trash can.

4.4 Resources

It is hard to specify the required resources without appreciating the volume of a project. For a medium-size project, however, the following is a typical set of resources.

Requirements Testing Team: Typically the number of team members is kept small to avoid unnecessary discussions; for a medium-size project the team is usually two to three members. But there must be enough experienced heads on the team to provide different perspectives on the same issues. The team is responsible for creating and exercising test cases. It is usually wise to include on the team at least one person who was part of the requirements collection. This provides the testing team with first-hand knowledge of the requirements and their actual meanings.

Quality Assurance Person: There must be one person on the team whose primary responsibility is to ensure the quality of the system. This person provides an outside view on the quality and completeness of the test cases.

Testing Monitoring Tool: A testing monitoring tool can provide the team with the ability to track requirements, assign test cases to each of the requirements, and identify the results of the test cases. For a small project, monitoring can be done without a formal tool. But as complexity of a project grows, tools become a necessity. Tools also have the ability to record and playback the test cases. This feature is extremely helpful for regression testing of an object-oriented project that is built using iterative and incremental approaches. The tool should also have the ability to track bugs reported during testing throughout their life cycle.

Primary Users: A small team of users is absolutely essential in testing requirements for a project. Members of this team should represent different types of users of the desired system. Review meetings should be held regularly with this team to validate, eradicate, and add requirements.

4.5   Effort

Testing requirements is an uphill task. The chaos during the requirements phase is not easy to deal with. Testing requirements in the chaos runs parallel with their collection. The testing team must meet with the users at least once a week, twice if possible. The time spent testing the requirements should be at least as much as the time spent collecting them. The weekly meetings with the users should continue not only through the requirements collection process but afterward as well. The test plan for a project must mention how much time and effort would be involved for the given project.

4.6   Acceptance Criteria

User satisfaction with the requirements is the major acceptance criterion. Users of the system must be satisfied that they have seen their wish list in concrete form. This wish list, however, must be feasible in the project time and economic framework. Analysts and testers should ensure that the users' wish list is feasible, uncontradictory, and unredundant. Analysts/testers achieve this goal via iterative reviews with the users. Once both parties agree with the functional requirements, performance requirements, quality requirements, domain object model, use cases, user interface, test cases, and prototypes, it is time to move on to the next macro phase of development.

4.7   Summary

The cost of the removal of software bugs is directly proportional to the length of time between their occurrence and their identification, called the *latency time*. Requirements testing helps detect the inadvertent bugs in a software system at an early stage. This not only reduces the cost of software development but also tends to deliver a software system closer to the scheduled time.

Requirements testing emphasizes three attributes of software requirements: correctness, completeness, and consistency. Singular and collective testing of these requirements characteristics is the key to a successful system. Due to the lack of commercial software testing tools, prototyping and feedback become very useful during software requirements testing.

5
Design Testing

Testing the validity of designs in not a novel concept; it is as old as design itself. Whenever we design something, we test it, at least mentally, to ensure that the design will meet its expectations.

Software design testing is no different from other design testing. Traditionally, software is tested only after it has been given a physical form in lines of code. The waterfall model of software development is a perfect example of this approach to testing. As object-oriented software development is maturing into an engineering discipline, more emphasis is being given to the testing of designs. The software development community is recognizing the importance of detecting defects during the earlier phases of software development life cycle. Design errors, in particular, are much more expensive than errors committed during the later stages. Therefore, it is imperative that an organization commit its best resources to the testing of software designs.

With the emergence of object-oriented technology, the activities and outcomes of the software design phase have changed. An object-oriented design is not a strict top-down design of the functionalities of a system. Object-oriented design results in a set of collaborating objects working together to achieve a common goal. The process of object-oriented design is inherently different from that of traditional approaches. D. Champeaux et al.[DLF93] categorize design into *functional, physical,* and *performance* design. In all three categorizes, there is no distinction between "coarse" and "detailed" design. These categories focus on the goals rather than on the granularities of the design. Performance design methods, for example, consider both large and small performance factors.

The fundamental differences between object-oriented and functional design approaches call for a cataclysm in design testing techniques. This chapter deals with the testing of object-oriented designs. Section 5.1 deals with the objective of testing during the design phase. This section details the products of the design phase and the rationale behind their testing. Approaches used to test these outputs of design phase are listed in section 5.2. The steps involved in implementing these testing techniques are described in section 5.3. Sections 5.4 and 5.5 describe the required resources and effort estimation for testing designs. Finally, section 5.6 describes the acceptance criteria for moving to the next phase of the software engineering life cycle.

5.1   Objective

The objective of the design phase is to generate complete specifications for implementing a system using a set of tools and languages. The design phase employs composition and refinement techniques to transform a set of requirements into a complete plan for implementing the system[DLF93].

The design stage inherits three types of requirements from the analysis stage, namely, *functional,resource,* and *performance* requirements[DLF93]. The process of object-oriented design transforms these requirements into a complete plan for implementing the system. The two primary products of an object-oriented design are a description of the architecture and descriptions of common tactical policies[Boo94]. The architecture of an object-oriented system can be described via class diagrams and object interaction diagrams. The tactical policies include security, error handling, fail-over and recovery, memory management, and so on.

Based on the products of the design phase, there are five primary objectives for testing an object-oriented design[YT86][Boe84]. Similar issues for testing of software architectures are discussed in [Tra96].

- **Consistency:** There is no such thing as a correct or incorrect design. Some designs, however, provide better solutions to a problem than others. We would prefer a consistent and inelegant design any day over an elegant yet inconsistent design. Inconsistent design is a source of major errors that are not discovered until the later stages when it is exorbitantly expensive to change earlier design decisions. These errors also cause nightmares for the maintenance teams. Thus the first objective of testing designs is to eliminate inconsistencies.
- **Completeness:** An important attribute of a good design is that it provides a complete solution to all the problems it is supposed to solve. A design solution that is articulate in terms of meeting the functional requirements of a system is useless if it does not meet the performance requirements of the system or if it cannot be mapped to the resource

requirements given to the design stage. Thus, the second objective of design testing is to ensure that the design meets all its functional, resource, and performance requirements.

- **Feasibility:** One attribute of a good design is that the solution is realizable. It must be possible to implement the design in the specificed time and economic framework of the project.
- **Correctness:** A design must solve the problem at hand. The elegance of a design is not a substitute for solving the problem as laid out by the specifications of the system. A design is correct if its input and output relation can be proved true or false.
- **Traceability:** A design is traceable if the terms in a design have antecedents in earlier specification. This is much easier to keep track of if design refinements are intrinsically keyed to the object-oriented analysis models[DLF93].

5.2   Approach

The major reason, why software people shy away from testing design is the complexity and the required effort. With object-oriented design techniques, the situation has gotten worse because of the lack of good approaches for testing object-oriented designs and the scarcity of good object-oriented design testing tools in the marketplace.

Design testing can be manual or automated, and both can be either simple or mathematical. Manual techniques include design reviews, design walk-throughs, and design inspections[WF84]. Some of the formal verification techniques are based on inductive assertions, function semantics, and explicit semantics[BM85]. Other mathematical techniques include static analysis[YT86], symbolic execution[DE82], and so on. Automated verification systems include the Boyer-Moore theorem prover[BM79], the Standard verifier[ILJ75], the Gypsy Verification Environment[Goo82], and the Edinburgh LCI system[Gea77]. Most of these techniques are based on traditional software systems and can be applied to parts of object-oriented software.

Most of these techniques are based on formal verification of software. For projects driven by rigorous schedules and deadlines, these techniques unfortunately fail to offer a pragmatic solution. Hence one has to revert to simple and manual techniques for testing designs until more formal approaches and tools become feasible to use.

Our general approaches for testing an object-oriented design during its evolution are *design walk-throughs* and *prototyping.*

5.2.1 Design Walk-Throughs

Design review with the rest of the team is a powerful mechanism for identifying design errors. It ensures that the designer(s) did not miss any functional, performance, or resource requirements. There are three possible approaches that can be taken for design testing using walk-throughs.

1. **Alternative Approaches in Design:** This approach critiques the design by asking the designer what other approaches have been considered and rejected. If an approach was rejected, the reasons for rejection should be reviewed. Using this approach, alternatives to each design decision are challenged and the best solution is selected. Team members may suggest some alternative solutions to a single design decision that may have been missed by the designer(s).

2. **Alternative Designs:** Another approach, highly recommended by Hetzel[Het88], is to find the best design through competition. In this approach, more than one design team is formed. Each team independently designs the system within a given time frame. At the end of this period, the designs are presented to a judging committee. The committee critiques the designs with the designers and assigns points to each design. The design with the maximum points wins. The greater win, of course, is for the project. Some of the good ideas from the rejected designs can be applied to the selected design.

   In our opinion, this is often not a pragmatic plan. Usually development teams are short of resources and cannot afford the luxury of multiple design teams. Even with the available resources, a project's time and economic framework may not permit a design competition. Also, not everyone is a good loser. If four design teams take part in a design competition, only one is going to be the eventual winner. This may leave a feeling of resentment among the members of the other three teams, which cause long-term problems for the project;the losing team members may unnecessarily criticize design decisions at each step of the development process.

3. **Test Designs Through Test Cases:** Another possible approach for testing designs is to create a set of test cases for each iteration of the design. The review team can walk through the design using the test cases to determine whether a certain design property conforms to the output of the test case. Such models are extensively used to test database design configurations, transaction sequences, response times, and user interfaces[Het88].

   Performance characteristics of a design caused the demise of many projects. Testcase-based design testing can be effectively used to test the performance model of an object-oriented design. Some of the other areas that can be explored through this approach are internal interfaces, complex paths or processes, and worst-case scenarios. Test cases do not have to emerge from the design itself; requirements-based test cases can be more effective[ROT89].

5.2.2 Prototyping

An effective design validity technique is to transform the design into a physical shape, a prototype. Prototyping serves many purposes during design.

- Prototyping gives a designer the ability to choose between many design alternatives. At each step of the way, a designer is faced with multiple design options. Through prototyping it is easier to pick the best alternative.
- Prototyping provides confidence in a designer's design decisions. If it were not for prototyping, a designer could never be sure that a certain design meets the required functional, performance, and especially the resource requirements of a system.
- Prototyping supports a designer's arguments about why a particular design decision was preferred. Prototyping unveils certain characteristics of a design property that were not otherwise obvious. These hidden attributes of a certain design decision aid in adopting or rejecting a specific design.
- Prototyping gives a designer the ability to physically see the behavior of a certain design property. A designer may have put too many buttons on the GUI part of the software. Unless it is given a physical form, the designers or the users may not be able to make a decision about the ergonomics of the system.
- Prototyping can discover erroneous design decisions at an early stage. One design defect can lead to a myriad of system errors.

5.3 Activities

Through modeling and simulation, it is possible to execute a design on a computer to analyze the functional, performance, and resource characteristics of the design structure[Per95]. An object-oriented software design is created by mapping the models created during the requirements analysis phase to the models that propose a solution to meet those requirements. The process of mapping one model to another can potentially introduce many errors in the software and must be thoroughly tested. The higher quality of object-oriented projects is usually a result of fewer mappings and transformations compared to other development approaches[MK94].

Object-oriented design is an iterative and incremental process that refines a solution with each cycle of the process. It is iterative in the sense that the architecture of the system is refined with each iteration. The

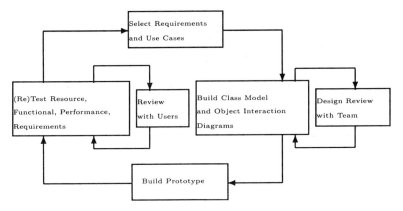

FIGURE 5.1. Object-Oriented Design Testing Process.

process is incremental in the sense that the architecture is incrementally expanded to provide solutions for more requirements with each incremental cycle[Boo96].

The process of testing object-oriented designs is very similar to the process of testing requirements. The primary difference between requirements and design testing lies in the focus and the outcome of each phase. Our object-oriented testing approach, interwoven with the object-oriented design process, is shown in figure 5.1.

The reader should look at figure 5.1 from a testing perspective. Our focus is on object-oriented design testing, not on the design process itself. Figure 5.1 shows one of the many possible ways a design process can be approached. It is not our intent here to promote a particular design process. Instead, we propose a testing process for any valid object-oriented design process. The details of the design process is a completely different subject and is out of the scope of this book. Readers interested in the details of the design process are referred to[DLF93], among many others.

5.3.1   Typical Activities in Design Testing

Formal and informal reviews of different products of the object-oriented design phase are the predominant methods of testing. The reviews determine the correctness, completeness, and consistency of a design. During the following typical set of activities, these attributes of design must be considered every step of the way. These activities are not to be followed religiously. Instead, they provide guidelines for testing object-oriented designs and can be modified based on the requirements of a project.

The details of each step involved in object-oriented design testing are given in figure 5.2 and are outlined in the following paragraphs. As mentioned earlier, this set of activities is repeated in an iterative manner until a complete and consistent solution has been provided, tested, and approved.

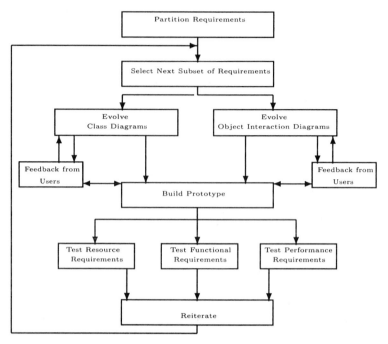

FIGURE 5.2. Object-Oriented Design Testing Activities.

1. **Partition the requirements:** The first step in object-oriented design testing is to select a subset of requirements. The partitioning of requirements is a typical classification problem and can be done in many ways. One possible categorization of these requirements may have been done during the analysis stage. The other possible way is to partition the requirements based on the *ensembles*[1] in a system. Yet another possibility is to break the requirements down by use cases. Each use case may have a set of associated requirements. All requirements associated with a use case belong to one set.

2. **Select Requirements Subset:** Selection of requirements for the given iteration is the next step in the design iteration. This selection is design dependent and will vary from system to system. Designers are the best judge for this selection. From the testing perspective, it should not impact the system. Testers should develop test sets based on the classification of the requirements. These test sets should be populated with appropriate test cases to validate the given subset of requirements.

3. **Select the Related Use Cases:** The selection of requirements drives the selection of associated use cases. There may be a many-to-many re-

---

[1]An *ensemble*[DLF93] is defined as *an object with other objects and/or subensembles as its functional constituents.*

lationship between a set of use cases and a set of requirements. This relationship may vary from project to project. The use cases drive the functional design testing and serve as the source for creating test cases for this design iteration. A subset of use cases associated with the requirements of the given design iteration are selected.

4. **Evolve/Review Design Class Model:** Once a set of requirements and use cases has been selected, designers create a class model. A class model represents the static model for the partial solution to the problem. It encompasses a set of classes, their attributes, and their interrelationships. A class design model is a representation of the solution to the problem represented by the domain object model. The class model is created by transforming the domain object model. The process of mapping one model to another is prone to error[MK94]. Testing of the class model is partially accomplished by comparing the design model with the analysis model. This comparison can be accomplished through internal team reviews initially and through external reviews later.

5. **Evolve/Review Object Interaction Diagrams:** Object interaction diagrams focus on messages dispatched between collaborating objects. They represent the dynamic aspect of the problem being solved. For a given subset of requirements, designers identify the required classes, data attributes, and methods. The objects created from these classes must collaborate with each other intelligently to satisfy a specific system requirement. An object interaction diagram is a tool that lets a designer depict the flow of messages between objects over time. While the logic for individual methods is hidden under the class interface, application logic is embedded in the object interaction diagrams. Designers must decide the invoked methods of individual classes, along with their order of invocation. One of the advantages of object interaction diagrams is that they clearly specify the flow of activity over time. They also allow an easier transformation of the design model to the implementation. This close relationship between the design model and the implementation tends to reduce the possibility of errors in the transformation.

Object interaction diagrams must be thoroughly tested. Object interaction diagram reviews serve as a big factor in eliminating errors in the design stages. The reviews should be performed on a formal basis. Generally two types of object interaction diagram reviews are performed, *internal reviews* and *external reviews*. Internal reviews are performed by the development team itself, while external reviews include the user community, as well. Each aspect of the design must be presented to the internal and external review committees. The *internal* review committee should include but should not be limited to designers working on the other aspects of the software, a domain expert, a coordinator, a testing expert, and a database expert. The external review committee should include the designer, representatives from user community, a tester, and a database expert.

The review committee members must look at the designs from the perspective of the role they are playing in the review meetings. A tester, for example, must look at the object interaction diagrams and determine test cases for the given requirements and use cases. The tester must use different testing techniques[2] to validate the requirements.

Designers should first ensure, through internal reviews, that they are solving the problem correctly. Some of the things to watch out for are the performance requirements, functional requirements, and resource requirements. Among others, concurrency and deadlock errors must also be considered[Pos87].

Additionally, designers must validate that they are solving the correct problem through external reviews with the users of the system. Although the users may have signed off on a requirements document, the dynamic nature of certain businesses does not guarantee a set of frozen requirements. This is why it is imperative that the users of a system be involved at each phase of development and testing. External reviews with the user community provide an outside perspective on the testing of the system. Testers should ask the users to think about how are they going to test the system. There are two advantages to this: (1) users are the best judge of how the system is going to be used in real life; (2) by thinking about the system testing, users provide the development team with a concrete set of testable requirements. Testers must include the feedback from users in their test plans and consequently in the test cases.

6. **Build a Prototype for the Given Partition:** An idea sometimes works on the back of an envelope and then coerces the designer to think about many other aspects once the same idea is given the form of code. Prototyping helps designers in testing their ideas as well as in opting for the best design decisions. Advantages of prototyping are discussed in section 5.2.2. From a testing perspective, the developed prototypes for the selected subset of requirements is shared with the users. Users are invited to provide feedback on the user interface of the system. They are also invited to play with the prototype to get a feel of the final application. This refines user requirements and expectations of the system. But from the testing perspective, the biggest advantage of a prototype is that the users and the testers can think clearly about testing the system for various types of requirements. Testers can build test cases for the end product based on their experience with the prototypes. The test cases are themselves tested by sharing with the users and by eliciting feedback. Users can provide very useful feedback in improving the quality of the test cases.

---

[2]Testing techniques may include *functional testing*, *boundary-value testing*, *cause-effect testing*, *event-directed testing*, and *state-directed testing*.

7. **Test the Resource Requirements:** For the selected subset of requirements, testers must create test cases to validate the requirements. These test cases in turn can be categorized into the types of requirements they are going to test. The first category of such test cases is resource test cases. Examples of such test cases include the maximum number of application windows open on a client machine, minimum amount of memory required to run the application, and concurrent execution of the system under development with other systems on the available set of resources.

   In many ways, prototyping tests the resource requirements of an end product. Testers must evaluate the resource requirements of the system and create test cases for them. Once the prototypes have been created, test cases are evaluated for their validity and appropriate changes are made.

8. **Test the Functional Requirements:** The second category in the test cases deal with the functional aspect of the system. System users are generally more interested in the observable behavior of the system. Again, based on the given subset of requirements, use cases, and the design, testers must create test sets and test cases. When a prototype for the given subset of requirements is created, the test sets must be tested in consultation with the users. User feedback is the most important element for functional testing and must be utilized to add, delete, or modify the designed test cases.

9. **Test the Performance Requirements:** Performance requirements of a system are the driving force for creating performance test cases of a system. Like the other two types of test cases, performance test cases must be designed during analysis and design stages. With the onset of a given iteration of prototype, the performance test cases can be executed on the prototype. The results of this execution, and the selected subset of requirements determine the amount of modifications to these test cases. Here, again, these test cases are validated through execution and through the users feedback.

10. **Reiterate:** At the end of each iteration, the design needs to be modified. Designers alter the design and proceed to the next iteration by going back to step 2. Inclusion of more requirements in the next iteration is dependent on the required design modifications.

5.4 Resources

A design team is generally small. According to Booch[Boo96],

> Design is best conducted by a small team made up of the project's very best people.

We complement this statement by adding that this small team must include a project's very best testing and quality assurance people. For a medium-size project, the following represents the testing and quality resource requirements in addition to the architect(s), toolsmith, database expert, network expert, and so on.

Design Testing Team: The team should include at least one test leader. The number of testers in each project will depend on the size of the design team. For each architect in the design team, there should be a test architect. If a project demands design by more than one team, there should be one test architect on each team. The test architect is responsible for providing conceptual integrity in the testing effort throughout the development process. One test architect can suffice for smaller projects. For medium to large projects, the test architect should be backed up by multiple testers.

Quality Assurance Person: In addition to the chief test architect, there must be another outside observer to monitor the quality of the project. This person is responsible for ensuring the quality of the project by monitoring the correctness and completeness of test cases, test sets, and schedules.

Technical Writer: A technical writer, in conjunction with the principal architect, is responsible for documenting the architecture of a system. The same technical writer also documents the test architecture with the chief test architect.

Test Monitoring Tool: An essential ingredient for a complete testing effort is a test monitoring tool. This tool provides testers with the cability to enter test sets, test cases, and the requirements the test cases cover. The test cases can be applied to the prototypes. The test cases can be recorded in the tool and played back with each new iteration of the design. A test monitoring tool also shrinks the regression testing effort considerably.

Users: A core group of users is an asset for delivering a quality product. The users must, however, be guided in turning their perspective from using the system to testing the system.

5.5   Effort

The success of a project relies heavily on its design. For an object-oriented project in particular, the best efforts of a team must be devoted to the design phase. Hence, the best testing resources and ample time should be committed to design testing. Testing of designs is not easy, however. There are no executables available till the prototypes are created. Testing of the transformation from analysis model to design model for completeness and correctness is mainly a manual process. Regular meetings must be held throughout the design phase with the users of the system. The frequency of these meetings varies with the design stage as well as with the size of the project. In the beginning, designers have to work independently to provide a solution to the given requirements. At such an early stage, designers tend to stay away from the users. However, regular meetings with the user community helps to avoid unnecessary assumptions made on the behalf of users as well as on behalf of designers. The meeting for both internal and external reviews must be regularized once the general framework of design has evolved.

5.6   Acceptance Criteria

Design of an object-oriented software system is never finished until the system is delivered[Boo96]. The development team must have enough confidence in the framework of the design, as well as in the design decisions and its associated risks, to move forward with a full-fledged implementation phase. This level of comfort is enhanced by testing. The testing team must have enough confidence that the test sets are complete, consistent, and correct. Completeness of test sets means that they cover all the functional, resource, and performance requirements of the system. Consistency of the test sets implies that for the same requirements no two test cases contradict each other. Finally, the correctness of test sets implies that the oracle has been correctly specified. As well as the design acceptance criteria, the above acceptance criteria for design testing must be met before moving into the next major phase of the project.

The high confidence level of the test team by itself does not suffice, however, to advance to the next macro phase of development. The confidence of the testing team must be validated by an approval stamp from the eventual users of the system.

5.7   Summary

Testing software designs warrants significant effort, commitment, resources, and a viable approach. Until recently there has been a scarcity of object-oriented software design testing approaches and tools. The lack of attention, however, is not due to the lack of need. The ever-increasing user expectations from software systems demand quality products in minimal time. One of the biggest potential strategies for increasing software quality is increasing the emphasis on software design testing.

Object-oriented software designs should be complete, correct, consistent, feasible, traceable, and testable. Only by testing these attributes of software designs can we meet the expectations of today's aware users. Ignoring design testing will only lead object-oriented software to the pitfalls that many other technologies seem to have fallen into.

6
Base Classes Unit Testing

The most significant impact on the testing of object-oriented software is the shift in focus to unit and integration testing strategies[Ove93a]. A `class` is the basic building block for constructing object-oriented software[PBC93]. Hence, it is the most natural unit of testing. The notion of a class as a unit of testing has been supported by many object-oriented project experience reports[MTW94]. Class-level testing requires substantial effort in the engineering of highly robust and reliable object-oriented systems. Testing of a `class` in an object-oriented system is not trivial, however. Most of the publicized features of object-oriented software have insidious effects on the application of conventional software testing approaches to unit testing.

Over the past ten years, many researchers and practitioners have dealt with issues related to the testing of object-oriented programs; see, for example,[Fie89] [Heg89] [PK90] [SR90] [FD90] [CM90] [HMF92] [TR92b] [MTW94] [Mar95] [GKH+95] [KGH+95b] [Bin96i] [CMLK96a] [Hun95b] [Hun96a] [Hun96b]. In this chapter, we present a generalized, ordered set of activities for testing a stand-alone `class`. These activities are specific for the C++ language, but the same concepts can be applied for class testing in any class-based object-oriented language.

6.1 Objective

Unit testing focuses on the verification of the smallest building blocks of software design[Pre97]. Unit testing assures that individual parts of a complex system work correctly in isolation, before their eventual integration. Although it is considered an excellent idea by many, unit testing is not widely and formally practiced. Various factors contribute toward this lack of formality. One of the most commonly observed factors is the lack of effort and commitment to unit testing. *Extensible* and *reusable* unit test cases are hard to build. As code for a unit changes, its test cases can become obsolete very quickly. Another factor is the lack of software management support for unit testing. Unit testing is not conceived as an explicit deliverable in a project. A developer may divert his or her attention to other more perceived deliverables of a project plan. More often than not, unit testing is then performed very informally. Test cases and test results are usually not maintained even if they are formally created. With the revelation of the possible advantages of unit testing, both management and development staff can change their attitude towards testing. Motivations and objectives for testing a class in isolation include the following[Hun96b]:

Correctness: One of the basic objectives of testing a class is to furnish confidence that the intended logic has been correctly encapsulated in the class. At a unit testing level, correctness of a class implies two types, correctness of behavior and correctness of implementation. Correctness of behavior again is of two types: (1) that the class delivers on the services that it promises to perform and (2) that the class responds elegantly in the face of unexpected conditions.

Correctness of implementation can be determined by asking two simple questions: (1) Does the code conform to its specifications[Het88]? and (2) Does the object deviate from its specified behavior? A class must correctly implement the proper logic inside each of its methods. These methods should in turn behave correctly in the face of both expected and unexpected signatures and object states. Test cases should be built for all possible states and signatures then.

Completeness: Another aspect of unit testing is to ascertain whether all the necessary logic is present in the class. Completeness of a class can be evaluated by asking three questions: (1) Does the class have all the necessary functions associated with it? (2) Is each necessary function available as the public interface of the class under test? (3) Does each method of a class completely execute its specified responsibility?

Early Testing: Unit testing provides an opportunity to test a class prior to its integration with other classes. Early bug discovery significantly reduces the cost of fixing bugs at the post design stages.

Easy Debugging: During unit testing, the scope of a bug is reduced to the class under test. If the same bug is found during integration or system testing, it is harder to localize it. Unit testing localizes a bug to a single class.

Better Coverage: Structural testing of a single class is easier as the possible traversable paths are usually not unlimited. Regardless of the selected coverage criterion, coverage of all possible paths is manageable at the unit level.

Better Regression Testing: Once a bug has been fixed in the class under test, it is easier to execute regression tests to verify that the fixed bug has not introduced any side effects.

Reduced Future Testing Effort: Unit testing provides confidence in the classes and objects during integration and system testing. During the later stages of testing, testers can focus on errors associated with integration and system testing.

Better Quality System: Most importantly, high quality components tend to give rise to high quality systems. Unit testing lends itself to better units, or classes in object-oriented software systems.

6.2 Approach

Adequately testing the individual methods in a class does not ensure that the class has also been adequately tested[MS92]. This conjecture has been supported by the extension of Weyuker's [Wey86] *anticomposition* axiom by Perry and Kaiser[PK90].[1] It implies that in addition to functional (specification-based) and structural testing, some other testing strategy is also warranted that not only tests the interaction of methods in a class but also considers the state of an object during testing. Functional testing validates the black-box view of methods in a class. Functional testing exercises a member function as a stand alone entity. Method-interaction testing, on the other hand, emphasizes the correct interaction of a member function of a class with other member functions and with data members of the class, while maintaining the integrity of its state.

Before proceeding further, let's look at a `class`, as proposed by C++ object model. A `class` encapsulates a set of data elements and provides a set of operations that can access the data elements. A class K can be defined as a tuple,

$$K = \langle D(K), M(K) \rangle,$$

where $D(K)$ and $M(K)$ are sets of data members and member functions, respectively, of class K, and are given by

$$D(K) = \{d_i \mid d_i @ K\},[2]$$

---

[1]Readers interested in these testing axioms and how our approach satisfies them are referred to appendix E.

[2]We use the @ symbol to denote the relationship between a class and its attributes, i.e, its data members and its member functions. Thus $i @ A$ means that a data member i is an attribute of class A.

$$M(K) = \{m_i \mid m_i \text{ @ } K\}.$$

There is no predefined order of invocation for methods in a class. Testing a `class` is equivalent to finding the sequence[3] of operations for which a class will be in a state that is contradictory to its axioms[SR92]. Testing a `class` for all possible sequences of methods is a resource-intensive activity in terms of both time and money, equivalent to *exhaustive* testing. The resources required to test a class also increase exponentially with the increase in the number of its methods. The number of all possible combinations to test for a class with 10 `public` methods, each with a single occurrence, is $3628800(= 10!)$. If each of these sequences takes a second to execute, it would require more than 1000 hours of computer time to test the combinations of only these 10 methods. Obviously software development team does not have such luxury of time for unit testing, necessitating a strategy that reduces number of sequences considerably and still provides an acceptable degree of confidence in the correctness of the class after testing. This chapter outlines a new approach that reduces the number of sequences substantially by judiciously exploiting the state of an object.

The state of an object at a single instance of time is equivalent to the aggregate state of each of its data members at that instance. Methods of a class manipulate this set of data members in various ways. The correctness of a class, therefore, depends on (1) whether the data members are correctly representing the intended state of an object and (2) whether the member functions are correctly manipulating the representation of the object.

Based on this theory of correctness, a `class` in an object-based system can be viewed as composition of a set of `slices`. A `slice` of a class can be defined as a quantum of a class with only a single data member and a set of member functions such that each member function can manipulate the values associated with this data member. A `slice`, associated with a data member d_i of a class K can be represented by

$$Slice_{d_i}(K) = \langle d_i, M_{d_i}(K) \rangle,$$

where

$d_i \in D(K)$

$M_{d_i}(K) = \{m_i \mid m_i @@ d_i\}$[4]

---

[3] A sequence *Seq* is defined as a nonempty, ordered set of methods of a class. A sequence is defined for a specific data member d_i of class K, and is part of a test case for d_i. Generally, a method will appear exactly once in a sequence. It can be denoted mathematically by

$$Seq(TC_{d_i}(K)) = seq_i \mid seq_i \in Perm(M_{d_i}(K)).$$

[4] The symbol @@ is employed to denote the usage relationship. Thus $m@@i$ represents the usage of data member i by method m.

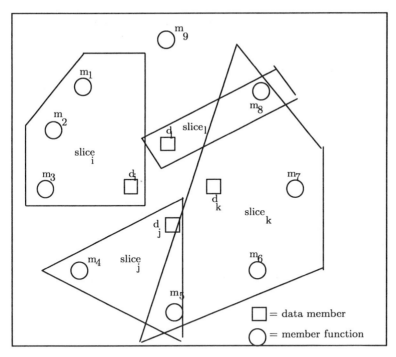

FIGURE 6.1. C++ `class` in terms of slices.

$$M_{d_i}(K) \subseteq M(K)$$

Thus a `class` is nothing but a composition of slices and functions. A class with n data members can be represented by

$$K = \{Slice_{d_1}, Slice_{d_2}, Slice_{d_3}, ..., Slice_{d_n}, Fns\},$$

where

$$Fns = \{f_i \mid f_i \in M(K) \text{ and } f_i \not\!\!\!\text{@} \not\!\!\!\text{@} d_i \in D(K)\}.[5]$$

A set of slices, when composed as a `class`, may have overlapping functions but each of them has a unique data member. A `class` in terms of slices is shown in figure 6.1.

Our unit testing strategy tests a `class` one `slice` at a time. Each `slice` in a class is associated with one unique data member and a subset of member functions. For as a single `slice`, its associated member functions are the only ones existing in this class. Testing all possible sequences of these methods is equivalent to testing the class for this slice or for this data member. Partial correctness of this subset of methods implies that these methods correctly manipulate the state of this data member. If a similar testing procedure is repeated for all slices of a class, then it can be concluded

---

[5] $\not\!\!\!\text{@} \not\!\!\!\text{@} \equiv$ inverse of @@

that all member functions of this class are correctly manipulating the state of an object of that type.

Our approach can be called a *hybrid* approach. Initially, we look at the implementation of a class to determine the subset of methods that are required to create sequences. Then we go a level of abstraction higher and test the class using a black-box approach.

6.3   Activities

The unit testing approach presented here can be called a *divide-and-conquer* strategy. We partition the state of an object into substates of each of its data members and then test the class based on each of these substates. Our approach is implemented using a set of ordered actions. These actions, or activities, are described in section 6.3.2. Before we go any further, however, we want to mention a few assumptions and constraints we use in our approach.

6.3.1   Assumptions

One of the foremost assumptions of our approach is that the employed compiler is correct and does not introduce any errors in the code by itself.

There are various levels of testing object-oriented software[Bas93]. In this chapter we focus on the unit-level testing of C++ programs. We test classes only as stand-alone entities; we do not consider the integration of classes into components, packages, or into subsystems here. Integration of classes is addressed in chapter 10.

Our testing strategy assumes a language that is a subset of C++. model We picked C++ because of its increasing popularity and its use in industry as well as in academia, and because of the wide variety of available tools. Some of the other assumptions that we considered about the language and about the environment are as follows.

- The language is strongly typed.
- The language uses static binding whenever possible for reasons of efficiency.
- The language supports three levels of visibility, *private, protected,* and *public* of the attributes of a class.
- The language supports single and multiple inheritance. This chapter discusses unit testing stand-alone base classes. Unit testing of derived classes is addressed in chapter 7.
- The developer of a class performs its unit testing.

// *Taken from libg++ and slightly modified.*

```
class TestSS;

class SampleStatistic {
friend Test;

    protected:
      int n;
      double x;
      double x2;
      double minValue, maxValue;

    public :
      SampleStatistic();
      virtual ~SampleStatistic();
      virtual void reset();

      virtual void operator+=(double);
      int samples();
      double mean();
      double stdDev();
      double var();
      double min();
      double max();
      double confidence(int p_percentage);
      double confidence(double p_value);

      void error(const char* msg);
};
```

FIGURE 6.2. Interface of the class under test.

6.3.2 Typical Activities in Unit Testing

A class contains a set of routines and a set of data structures that represent the state of an object of that class. In C++, the set of routines associated with a class is known as its *methods*. Although the methods may perform according to specifications individually, they may elicit incorrect behavior in the presence of other methods of the same class. The errors effected by this interaction of methods must be tested here. A step-by-step procedure for unit testing a simple class `SampleStatistic`, from *GNU*'s g++ library[Lea92], is illustrated in the following pages. The interface of the class is shown in figure 6.2.

This class has 11 public member functions, 1 constructor, 1 destructor, and 5 data members. It also uses some external functions, which are assumed to be correct. If the class is tested for all possible combinations of methods, with each method appearing in a sequence exactly once, then one would have to test $(11)!$, which is equivalent to 39916800, possible sequences of the 11 member functions. Our approach, however, reduces this number to about 5100.

Draw Enhanced Call-Graph (ECG)

Generally, a `call-graph` is employed to graphically represent the possible invocation of member functions of a class by its other member functions. In a call-graph, nodes represent methods of a class, whereas the edges denote the invocation of a method by another method of the same class. We enhance a `call-graph` by adding the direct usage of data members by each of the member functions, hence the name Enhanced Call Graph *(ECG)*. The *ECG* of a class K can be given by a 4-tuple,

$$ECG(K) = \langle M(K), D(K), E_{md}, E_{mm} \rangle,$$

where $M(K)$ and $D(K)$ are as defined on page 51:

$E_{md} = \{(m_i, d_j) \mid$ there is an edge between m_i and $d_j\}$
$E_{mm} = \{(m_i, m_j) \mid$ there is an edge between m_i and $m_j\}$.

After reviewing the interface and the implementation, as given in appendix A, of `SampleStatistic` class, its ECG is given in figure 6.3. The small circles and squares represent the member functions and data members, respectively, of `SampleStatistic` class.

Draw Minimal Data Members Usage Matrix (MaDUM)

An ECG represents the usage or invocation of members of a class by the other members. We want to observe more closely this relationship between data members and member functions. Based on ECG, we draw a matrix, called a minimal data-members-usage matrix (MaDUM).

A MaDUM is an $n \star m$ matrix, where n is the number of data members in the class and m represents the number of member functions in the class. An entry $MaDUM_{i,j}$ is marked for the correct usage type if the jth member function manipulates ith data member in its implementation. This matrix gives a visual feeling of the usage of a given data member by a subset of methods. It also gives a crude measure of the *cohesion* of the class:

$$MaDUM_l(i,j) = \begin{cases} t_l & \text{if method } j \rightsquigarrow \text{ data member } i \\ r_l & \text{if } j \text{ reports the state of } i \\ o_l & \text{if } j @@ i \\ & \text{else} \end{cases}$$

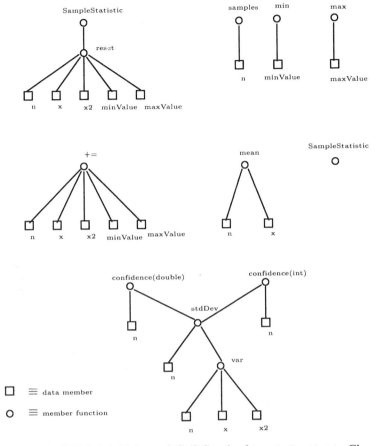

FIGURE 6.3. Enhanced Call Graph of SampleStatistic Class.

where $\leadsto \equiv transforms$[6] and l is the level at which member function j manipulates data member i. The value of level l is 1 if j directly uses i.

Drawing a MaDUM may not be so obvious as it may seem initially. A data member may be accessed by a member function *indirectly*, i.e, through invoking another member function of the same class. It is not unusual for a member function to invoke only another member function, called a *helper* function, to do something on its behalf.[7] A member function may not access any data member of its class directly; instead it accesses them through its *helper* functions. If the only statement in a `caller` method is to invoke a *helper* function, then for all practical purposes the effect of calling either

---

[6]We are using $\leadsto$ symbol to denote the transformation relationship. Thus $m \leadsto d$ expresses that the method m can potentially transform the value of data member d.

[7]*Helper* member functions are known as *wrapper* member functions.

of these functions is essentially the same. Such redundant entries in the MaDUM should be removed. A complete algorithm for drawing MaDUM of a class is given in appendix D.

A MaDUM is also a useful indicator of the usability and testability metrics of a class. For example, the following can be determined from the MaDUM of a class.

- A row with no entries clearly indicates the violation of information hiding principles. A row represents a data member of a class. A data member not being utilized by any member function of a class implies that it is being utilized explicitly by the external agents. Unless it is needed, a row without entries should be reconsidered.
- A column with no entries may indicate that the member function does not belong to the class under test. A column represents a member function of a class. If a member function does not utilize any data member of the class under test, it may indicate that the member function has been retrofitted into the class. An empty column warrants reconsideration in terms of the class membership of a function. Sometimes a column with no entries is necessary in a class. For example, a class may have a method named *printErrorText(String errorText)*. This method takes an `errorText` *String* and prints it on the standard display.
- If a MaDUM can be broken down in such a way that one subset of data members exclusively uses a subset of member functions, then the subset of data members and their associated functions are candidates for a separate class. A class represents a unique concept or entity in a system. If more than one concept or entity has been coerced into one class, then its MaDUM can be broken down in the way described earlier. Breaking the class into multiple classes will enhance the testability and simplicity of the class.
- A row with more than five transformer entries may indicate a case of overdecomposition: the work may have been broken down into more methods than are necessary. This combination of methods should be revisited to consider combining one with another.
  Overdecomposition results in an exponential increase in unit testing efforts. Addition of a single method to a class enhances the required number of test cases exponentially. Developers must strike a balance between long methods and overdecomposition. One rule of thumb can be that if a private method does not have a potential reuse, then probably it does not deserve to be a separate method.

We employ the procedure outlined in appendix D to create MaDUM for `SampleStatistic` class.

1. Initialize: Let

$$K = SampleStatistic$$

Then

$$G(K) = \langle M, D, E_{md}, E_{mm} \rangle,$$

where

$M = Setofmemberfunctions$
$\quad = \{SampleStatistic, reset, + =, samples, mean, stdDev, var$
$\qquad min, max, confidence(int), confidence(double), error\}$

$D = Setofdatamembers$
$\quad = \{n, x, x2, minValue, maxValue\}$

$E_{md} = Directusageofdatamembersbymemberfunctions$
$\quad\; = \{(reset, n), (reset, x), (reset, x2), (reset, minValue),$
$\qquad (reset, maxValue), (+ =, n), (+ =, x), (+ =, x2),$
$\qquad (+ =, minValue), (+ =, maxValue), (mean, n), (mean, x),$
$\qquad (samples, n), (min, minValue),$
$\qquad (max, maxValue), (confidence(int), n),$
$\qquad (confidence(double), n), (stdDev, n),$
$\qquad (var, n), (var, x), (var, x)\}$

$E_{mm} = Directusageofmemberfunctionsbyothermemberfunctions.$
$\quad\;\; = \{(SampleStatistic, reset), (confidence(int), stdDev)$
$\qquad (confidence(double), stdDev), (stdDev, var)\}$

$U = Setofmemberfunctionsthatdirectlyuseatleast$
$\qquad onedatamember$
$\quad = \{reset, + =, mean, samples, min, max,$
$\qquad confidence(int), confidence(double), stdDev, var\}$

Cardinalities of these sets can be given by.

$$n_m = 12$$
$$n_d = 5$$
$$n_u = 10$$
$$i = 0$$

	Sample-Stat.	re-set	+=	sam-ples	mean	std-Dev	var	min	max	con-fid. (int)	con-fid. (dbl)	error
n		t_1	t_1	r_1	o_1	o_1	o_1			o_1	o_1	
x		t_1	t_1		o_1		o_1					
x2		t_1	t_1				o_1					
minValue		t_1	t_1					r_1				
maxValue		t_1	t_1						r_1			

FIGURE 6.4. First-Level DUM for `SampleStatistic` Class.

	Sample-Stat.	re-set	+=	sam-ples	mean	std-Dev	var	min	max	con-fid. (int)	con-fid. (dbl)	error
n	t_2					o_2				o_2	o_2	
x	t_2					o_2						
x2	t_2					o_2						
minValue	t_2											
maxValue	t_2											

FIGURE 6.5. Second-Level DUM(i=1) for `SampleStatistic` Class.

2. **Create First-Level DUM:** The first-level DUM, with appropriate types of data usage, is given in figure 6.4.
3. **Create Next-Level DUMs:** While U is not empty, create the next-level usage DUMs by readjusting U such that each member of U_{new} is a parent of some member of U_{old}.

For iteration $i = 1$, U is updated and is given by

$$U = \{SampleStatistic, confidence(int), confidence(double), stdDev\}$$

For iteration $i = 1$, DUM_i is given in figure 6.5.

For iteration $i = 2$, U is updated and is given by

$$U = \{confidence(int), confidence(double)\}$$

For $i = 2$, DUM_i is given in figure 6.6.

For iteration $i = 3$, $U = \emptyset$.
4. **Combine All DUMs:** By combining all DUM_is, we get the DUM given in figure 6.7.
5. **Minimize DUM:** For data member n, all branches with n as a leaf are given in figure 6.8.

	Sample-Stat.	re-set	+=	sam-ples	mean	std-Dev	var	min	max	con-fid. (int)	con-fid. (dbl)	error
n										o_3	o_3	
x										o_3	o_3	
x2										o_3	o_3	
minValue												
maxValue												

FIGURE 6.6. Third-Level DUM(i=2) for SampleStatistic Class.

	Sample-Stat.	re-set	+=	sam-ples	mean	std-Dev	var	min	max	con-fid. (int)	con-fid. (dbl)	error
n	t_2^R	t_1	t_1	r_1	o_1	$o_1 o_2$	o_1			$o_1 o_2 o_3$	$o_1 o_2 o_3$	
x	t_2^R	t_1	t_1		o_1	o_2^R	o_1			o_3^R	o_3^R	
x2	t_2^R	t_1	t_1			o_2^R	o_1			o_3^R	o_3^R	
minValue	t_2^R	t_1	t_1					r_1				
maxValue	t_2^R	t_1	t_1						r_1			

FIGURE 6.7. Union of all DUM_is of SampleStatistic Class.

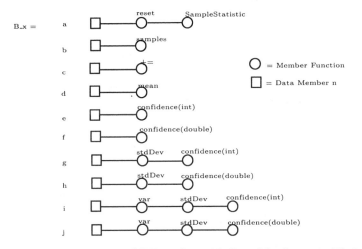

FIGURE 6.8. All Branches with Data Member n as Their Leaf.

Now for a

$$DUM[n][reset] \approx DUM[n][SampleStatistic]$$
$$\longrightarrow DUM[n][SampleStatistic] = Redundant(R).$$

For b, c, e, and f, there is no second level, so these entries are an essential part of MaDUM.

For g and h,

$$DUM[n][stdDev] \not\approx DUM[n][confidence(int)],$$
$$DUM[n][stdDev] \not\approx DUM[n][confidence(double)],$$

so these entries are nonredundant.

Similarly for i and j,

$$DUM[n][var] \not\approx DUM[n][stdDev],$$
$$DUM[n][stdDev] \not\approx DUM[n][confidence(int)],$$
$$DUM[n][stdDev] \not\approx DUM[n][confidence(double)],$$

so these entries are nonredundant.

On the same principle, all the redundant entries are marked in a DUM, shown with a letter R in figure 6.7.

6. **Remove Redundant Entries:** After removal of redundant entries from the DUM, the minimal DUM is created and is given in figure 6.9. Here each multiple entry has been changed to a single entry and the information about usage level is ignored.

Categorize Member Functions

The set of member functions of a class can be divided into four broad categories. This division is similar to the one in[Jal87].

- *Constructors* are functions that create values of a given type. A constructor is recognized by having the same name as the class itself.
- *Reporters* are operations that report the substate of an object. These functions do not change the state of the object in any way. The member functions are also known as *inspectors*.
- *Transformers* are operations that effect the state of the object in one way or the other. They operate on one or more data members of the

	Sample-Stat.	re-set	+=	sam-ples	mean	std-Dev	var	min	max	confi-dence (int)	confi-dence (dbl)	error
n		t	t	r	o	o	o			o	o	
x		t	t		o		o					
x2		t	t				o					
minValue		t	t					r				
maxValue		t	t						r			
	C	T	T	R	O	O	O	R	R	O	O	O

FIGURE 6.9. MaDUM for SampleStatistic Class.

class and change their values. Another name for these member functions is *mutators*.

- *Others* are operations that do not fall in any of the above categories. The most prominent of these is a *destructor* operation. Similarly, a `printError(char*)` functions also does not fall into any of the above categories.

Our approach tests a class one `slice` at a time. Let us say that we are testing for a given data member d_i. The `slice` for d_i is given by $Slice_{d_i}$ and the interface supported by $Slice_{d_i}$ is given by

$$M_{d_i}(K) = \langle R_{d_i}, C, T_{d_i}, O_{d_i} \rangle,$$

where

$R_{d_i} = \{r_{d_i} \mid r_{d_i} \text{ is a reporter method for data-member } d_i\}$

$C = \{c_i \mid c_i \text{ is a constructor of class } K\}$

$T_{d_i} = \{m_{d_i} \mid m_{d_i} \notin R_{d_i} \text{ and } m_{d_i} \notin C, \text{ and } m_{d_i} \leadsto d_i\}$

$O_{d_i} = \{o_{d_i} \mid o_{d_i} @@ d_i, \text{ and } O_{d_i} \notin R_{d_i}, \text{ and } O_{d_i} \notin C, \text{ and } O_{d_i} \notin T_{d_i}\}$

Each row in the MaDUM was marked with appropriate data usage type in the previous step. In this step, we distinguish the *constructors* in the MaDUM. The data usage entries in each column, representing *constructors* of the MaDUM, are changed from x to c. All the entries in the MaDUM are changed such that information about the level at which data were used is ignored. Thus each entry x_i is changed to x.

The last row in figure 6.9 gives the type of each method. "R" stands for reporter methods, "T" for transformers and "O" for any other methods. Here we also mark the constructor because it needs special testing.

Create a Test Class

Next, we create a class `Tester` that plays a significant role in determining the correctness of the class under test. Two of the major motivations for creating a `Tester` class are (1) to validate existing *reporter* methods and (2) to furnish *reporter* methods for data members that have no reporters associated with their respective slices.

`Tester` class is declared as a `friend` in the class to be tested. This allows `Tester` class to access the private data members of the class being tested. For each *reporter* method in the class being tested, an equivalent method is created in `Tester` class. `Tester` class, obviously, should also declare an object of the type class-under-test as one of its data members.

For our running, example we create a test class called `TestSS` that is declared a friend in the `SampleStatistic` class. The interface of the `TestSS` class is shown in figure 6.10.

The *permutation* member function takes an array of strings and generates all possible permutations of this array of strings. The user can also create

```
class TestSS{
    SampleStatistic* ss;
  public:
    TestSS(SampleStatistic* s):ss(s){}
    ~TestSS() {delete ss;}

    int samples() { return ss→n; }
    double min() { return ss→minValue; }
    double max() { return ss→maxValue; }
    double x() { return ss→x; }
    double x2() { return ss→x2; }

    void checkn();
    void checkmin();
    void checkmax();

    void permutation(String*, int total, int fst, int last, ostream
outFile);
    void append(String&, ostream);

};
```

FIGURE 6.10. Interface of TestSS Class

a permutation of the subarray by providing the starting and ending index in the array for which permutation is required. The *permutation* member function is used for generating the test sequences.

The following steps are used to test each `slice` of a class individually.

Test the Reporters

The first category of methods to be tested is the *reporter* type. First a very simple test should be performed on a *reporter* method. The *reporter* method of the object under test should be executed to ensure that the *reporter* method has not altered the state of the data member it is reporting on.

Once the state-preserving behavior of a *reporter* method has been ascertained, it is ready for more stringent testing. We create a random sequence of operations of the `slice` under test and append it with the *reporter* method. We also append the same sequence with the corresponding method of `Tester` class. Our claim is that the results of the *reporter* method and of its *sibling* in `Tester` class should be same. This can determine the correctness of a *reporter* method according to its specifications. This strategy is powerful in the sense that the validity of a *reporter* method does not depend on the correctness of the sequence of operations that were invoked on the object before it. A *reporter* method should truly report the state of the data member it is responsible for. Replicating such reporter service in `Tester` class gives us confidence in the original *reporter* method. Further testing of the *reporter* method can be continued by invoking it after different sequences of operations. One can create all possible permutations of the methods, except the *reporter*s, of a slice. Each *reporter* of the `slice` is then tested for each sequence.

The reporter for data member n is *samples*. There are seven member functions, other than *samples*, that use n. We create some random sequences of these member functions. At the end of each sequence, we invoke the *checkn* of `TestSS` object. This method determines whether the value of n reported by *samples* matches the actual value. About 100 different sequences were tried and *checkn* always reported matching results.

Similarly, *min* and *max* were also tested, and it was determined that they correctly reported the values of `minValue` and `maxValue`, respectively.

Test the Constructors

The next category of methods to be tested is the *constructor* type. Constructors in a class can be easily identified since they have the same name as the class itself. Constructors are essentially the initializing functions for an object. They initialize various data members of a class according to their implementation.

Testing the *constructor* of a class consists of testing two essential properties: (1) all data members are correctly initialized and (2) all data members are initialized in correct order.

As stated earlier, our approach to testing a class is from a single data member's perspective. A *constructor* is assumed to initialize a data member to a specific value. To validate the first property of a *constructor*, we want to know if the *constructor* is initializing a data member to the correct value. Thus we append the *reporter* method of this data member, either from class-under-test or from `Tester` class, to the *constructor* and execute the sequence. Both types of *reporter*s are valid, so we trust their results to check the correctness of a *constructor*.

A constructor can be declared correct after it has been validated for all slices of a class. All the constructors of a class can now be tested employing the same approach.

The second property of a constructor to be tested may not be very obvious. Scott Meyers[Mey92] has shown that this can be a very common mistake in the constructor of a class and must be checked here. Our approach takes care of this problem since a constructor is completely executed before the state of the data member under test is checked. Any change in the initialization value of the data member under test would be caught here.

There is only one constructor for `SampleStatistic` class and all it does is call the *reset* member function. Thus we can say that the constructor and *re-*

set member functions are functionally equivalent. An empty column for the constructor in figure 6.9 reflects that the constructor for `SampleStatistic` class may not require testing. Thus no testing is required for the constructor in this case. The correctness of the constructor will be implicit after the member function *reset* has been tested.

Test the Transformers

Most of the remaining methods in a class can potentially transform the state of the data member a `slice` represents. We can put the remaining nontested methods in the same category.

Let us say the currently selected `slice` is $Slice_{d_i}$. Let the methods associated with this `slice` be M_{d_i}. Since we have already tested the *reporters* and *constructors*, the remaining methods to be tested can be given by M'_{d_i}. Then

$$M'_{d_i} = M_{d_i} - (R_{d_i} \cup C).$$

We create sequences of all possible permutations of the methods in M'_{d_i} such that each method appears in a sequence exactly once. These sequences represent possible ways in which this data member may be transformed. We append each of these sequences with the *reporter* method for the slice, i.e., for the data member. Thus if the cardinalities of M'_{d_i} and C are r and c, respectively, then the total number of sequences to be tested for this data member would be $c \star (r!)$. This is the upper bound on the number of test sequences.

In this step we are testing whether a given `slice` is being manipulated correctly by its *transformer* and *other* member functions. In a given member function, there may be multiple paths of execution. Manipulation of a `slice` under test could be present in more than one of these execution paths. It is the responsibility of the tester to ensure that the path(s) in which the `slice` is being manipulated is executed.

Each test sequence here consists of the *transformers* and *others*. If implemented correctly, *other* member functions should not transform the state of a given slice. Thus the only members that can alter the state of a `slice` are it *transformers*. A tester is responsible for creating such conditions that the execution path in which a `slice` under test is altered is exercised. This would ensure that a *transformer* function is exercised with the correct intention of altering the state of the slice. Once this state has been changed, it is easier for the tester to determine if the state alteration is according to the specification of the *transformer*.

The result of each of the preceding sequences can be compared with the expected result of the sequence. If the actual result matches the expected one, then we ignore that sequence of operations. On the other hand, if the result of a sequence of operations does not tally with the expected one, we know that at least one of the operations in the sequence is not performing according to its specifications. The sequence is then reduced by eliminating one method at a time and then reexecuting the sequence. This elimination strategy can localize the error to a specific method.

For $slice_n$, seven member functions need to be tested. Then we create all 5040 possible permutations of these seven member functions. Each of these sequences is appended by a statement to check whether n has been transformed according to the specification. The result of all these sequences is also found to be correct.

Test the Rest

As mentioned earlier, some member functions do not strictly fall into any of the three kinds of C++ class methods we have tested. For that matter, they may not even use any of the data members of a class they are part of. Consider, for example, a member function that prints an error string. It takes the error string as an argument and just prints it. Strictly speaking, it neither reports the state of any data member nor transforms the state in any way.

At this point, we are left with this kind of member function, if any. We propose that these member functions should be tested as if they are any other functions. It has already been determined that these functions are not affecting the state of the object. This conclusion has been drawn after testing the sequences affecting each data member of a class. The effect of these member functions in context of the rest of the member functions of the class has also been determined to be satisfactory. Thus, the only attribute of such functions that needs to be checked is their functionality as stand-alone entities. Any testing strategy for functional software can be used to test the correctness of these member functions.

At this point we have faith in all those member functions that can potentially affect the state of an object of type `SampleStatistic`. But we still have some member functions that should be tested for their functionality. One thing we do know about these functions is that they do not affect the state of the object of that class. Thus, we test these functions individually as stand-alone functions to determine their correctness. All of these remaining functions are also found to be correct.

Mutated `SampleStatistic` Class

To make our example more interesting, we induced an error in one of the transformer member functions. On line 1 of the $+=$ member function, we changed the statement

```
n += 1;
```

to

```
n =+ 1;
```

While testing for transformer member functions of n, the error was immediately discovered.

6.3.3 Analysis

This section provides a crude mathematical analysis of our testing strategy. Specifically, we develop expressions to calculate the number of test cases needed to test a given class.

Let us assume a class A such that

$$A = \langle M(A), D(A) \rangle.$$

Let us denote *cardinality* of a set G by $\sharp(G)$. Then we can assume that

$\sharp(M(A)) = num_m$
$\sharp(D(A)) = num_d$.

For a given data member d_i of class A, let

$M_{d_i}(A) = \langle R_{d_i}, C, T_{d_i}, O_{d_i} \rangle$
$\sharp(R_{d_i}) = num_r$
$\sharp(C) = num_c$
$\sharp(T_{d_i}) = num_t$
$\sharp(O_{d_i}) = num_o$

Also let us define a set $M'_{d_i}(A)$

$$M'_{d_i}(A) = \{T_{d_i} \cup O_{d_i}\}.$$

Then

$\sharp(Perm(M'_{d_i}(A))) = (\sharp(M'_{d_i}(A)))!$
$\sharp(Perm(M'_{d_i}(A))) = (\sharp(T_{d_i}) + \sharp(O_{d_i}))!$
$\sharp(Perm(M'_{d_i}(A))) = (num_t + num_o)!$

This number gives the total number of sequences to be executed to test the *transformer* methods of a class. The number of test cases for the *reporter* method(s) of a data member d_i is also given by the same number. For *slice*$_{d_i}$ of a class A, the total number of test cases to be executed to test the *reporters*, *transformers*, and *constructors* is given by

$$\sharp(TS_{d_i}(A)) = \sharp(Perm(M'_{d_i}(A))) + \sharp(Perm(M'_{d_i}(A))) \star (\sharp(C)) + \sharp(C)$$

$$\sharp(TS_{d_i}(A)) = (num_t + num_o)! + (num_t + num_o)! \star (num_c) + num_c$$

Since generally $\sharp(C) \ll \sharp(Perm(M'_{d_i}(A)))$, the above equation can be rewritten

$$\sharp(TS_{d_i}(A)) = ((num_t + num_o)!)(1 + num_c).$$

Hence, the total number of test cases to be executed to test a class can be written

$$\sharp(TS(A)) = \sum_{i=1}^{num_d} \sharp(TS_{d_i}(A)).$$

Using our technique, this is the upper bound on the number of test cases for a given class A. Not all the test cases are unique, but the intent of each of the test cases is unique. For example, all the sequences used to test the transformation of a data member can also be used to check the *reporter* method of the data member. Similarly, if the *transformer* set of a data member is equal to the *transformer* set of another, then the same sequences can be used to test both data members.

6.4 Resources

Unit testing is typically performed by the person who has developed the unit. The prerequisite for unit testing is the motivation to improve the quality of the unit[Het88]. It is widely argued that testing should be done by an independent person, a person other than the developer. While in principle this makes sense, it is not a pragmatic solution at the unit testing level. For all practical purposes, unit testing will have to be performed by its developer. We expect developers to be professional software engineers who understand their obligations towards developing quality software. Unit testing is part of this software development and must be performed completely and honestly.

Typically, the following resources are required during unit testing:

Test Case Documentation Tool: A tool that can be used to record the unit-level test cases.

Test Execution Tool: An automated tool is extremely helpful, especially for applications using graphical user interfaces (GUIs).

Storage Mechanism: A database or some other storage mechanism to save the test cases associated with a class. These test cases can later be reused for regression testing[KGH+95c][RH94] and for unit testing derived classes.

Requirements: A class must be tested against its requirements. The requirements must be available to the tester for specification-based testing.

Design: The design, documented in some form, must also be available for creating and executing design-based test cases.

Sample Data: It is always better to use real-world data to test a class. The data can be mutated to test boundary values for inputs, outputs, and the internal state of the class.

Coverage Tool: Depending on the type of code coverage, a tool executing the coverage can aid in effective unit testing.

6.5   Effort

Object-oriented technology provides many opportunities for errors to creep into a software. It has been proven that adequately testing the methods of a class in isolation does not ensure that a class has been adequately unit tested. A class should be tested at three different levels.

Functional Testing of Methods: The methods of a class should be tested for their functionality, ignoring their implementation. Each method should be tested in isolation. Functional testing of units should include boundary-value testing of input and output parameters. Any specification-based testing approach[HS96][Bei95] can be used for the functional testing of methods of a class.

Structural Testing of Methods: All the methods of a class should also be tested in isolation for a selected coverage criterion. A developer should ensure that values for the parameters are selected to ensure that all possible paths in a method are taken. Again, any code coverage technique[CMLK96a] can be employed for structural testing of these methods.

Interaction Testing of Method: Once the methods of a class have been tested in isolation, the interaction of the methods must be tested. A method is not a stand-alone entity anymore. The behavior of a method depends not only on the values of the input parameters but also on the state of the object the method is associated with. Hence the values of the data attributes of the class are also a very significant implicit input parameter to a given method. Since methods can change the values of the data attributes of an object, the order of invocation of methods can elicit different behaviors from that object. Hence, a developer/tester must try different orders of invocation of the methods on a class to determine an inconsistent behavior.

6.6   Acceptance Criteria

Acceptance criteria for a unit are determined by developer/tester. When a developer is satisfied with a unit, it is accepted as part of a system. The developer should request the assistance of a quality assurance expert for guidance in unit testing. Microsoft Corporation, for example, employs a testing buddies system where there is one-to-one ratio between developers and testers[CS96]. The developer/tester of a unit is responsible for ensuring that a class has been adequately tested. Adequate testing implies that the class has been tested at all three levels, i.e, methods functional testing, methods structural testing, and methods interaction testing. The tester must also ensure that all test cases, associated test data, and their execution results have been documented and are available for retrieval at a future time.

6.7 Summary

The enhanced call graph (ECG) and the minimal data member usage matrix (MaDUM) are keystones to our testing approach. They describe the relationship between the members of a class. This relationship is exploited in our semiexhaustive approach to unit testing a C++ class. Test cases are generated based on the meaningful sequence of methods. To make testing manageable, a class is broken down into slices and each slice is tested individually. Case studies show the usefulness of this approach.

The test procedure described here provides a tester with test sets that need to be executed on an object to ensure that the state of the object is manipulated correctly by its member functions. It does not tell the tester what values of input parameters, for example, should be used for a particular member function; such decisions are at the tester's discretion. This approach gives some general guidelines as to which logical states may be more important to test. The test cases, however, remain the ones that have been determined by this approach.

7

Derived Classes Unit Testing

Inheritance is one of the bases of object-oriented programming. Inheritance is a hierarchical relationship that allows us to exploit the commonality between various classes. Since classes represent concepts, and concepts do not exist in isolation, it can be implied that there is a logical relationship between various classes[Str91]. Inheritance is one of many possible glues that logically bind two classes. Inheritance provides a simple, flexible, and efficient mechanism for defining a new class by adding or modifying the facilities provided by an existing class. When two classes are related by inheritance, a class is *derived* from another class, which is then called a *base* class. The *derived* class inherits the properties, including data members and member functions, of its *base* class[ES90].

This chapter deals with the unit testing of inherited, or derived, classes. There are two extreme options for testing a derived class. One is to test a derived class as a *flattened*[1][BB91] class. This, however, would require retesting of all attributes of a base class. The other extreme possibility is to do the obvious. Apparently, if a base class has been adequately tested, then its attributes in a derived class need not be retested. This intuition has been rebutted.[PK90].

We contest that not all attributes of a base class need retesting in a derived class. Our solution identifies only the attributes of a base class

---

[1]According to Meyer[Mey90], the "*flattened* form of a class is the text of the class with the same features as the original, but with no inheritance clause. Features inherited directly or indirectly are put in the *flattened* form at the same level as the features declared locally."

that mandate retesting in a derived class scope. We assume that the base class has been adequately tested and the test history of the base class is available.

Here we deviate from our regular chapter format, i.e., *objective, approach, activities,* and so on. Although we are still addressing the unit testing of a class in an object-oriented or in an object-based language, the testing of derived classes is a significant topic and warrants serious consideration. In this chapter, we describe our approach toward testing derived classes. All recommendations and practices of chapter 6 are still applicable. '

7.1   Test Procedure

In chapter 6, we examined a procedure for testing a stand-alone class. Generating the test cases included *slic*ing the class and then generating test cases for each of the slices. In this chapter, we use the same test procedure to test a derived class $D_{derived}$. We assume that the base class B_{base} of class $D_{derived}$ has already been tested as a stand-alone class using the approach described in chapter 6. We introduce a notation by which an attribute of a class is subscripted with the *base* or *derived* keywords to identify the context in which it is being used.

We apply our `SampleStatistic` class test procedure to `SampleHistogram` class, a derived class of `SampleStatistic` class, in libg++[Lea92]. The interface of the class `SampleHistogram` is given in figure 7.1.

7.1.1   Draw Derived Enchanced Call Graph (ECG_{derived})

The first step in testing a derived class is to explicitly determine the inter- and intra- relationships between its local and inherited attributes. An ECG gives us a visual feeling of these relationships. We use the notation given in figure 7.2 to distinguish between the attributes of base and derived classes.

An ECG of `SampleHistogram` class is shown in figure 7.3.

7.1.2   Draw MaDUM_{derived}

The testing of a derived class starts with extending the MaDUM of its base class. Hence, the next step in testing a derived class is to draw its minimal data members usage matrix ($MaDUM$).

- Take the MaDUM of the base class B_{base}.

class SampleHistogram : **public** SampleStatistic
{
protected:
    short howManyBuckets;
    int *bucketCount;
    double *bucketLimit;

public:

    SampleHistogram(**double** low, **double** hi, **double** bucketWidth = -1.0);

    ~SampleHistogram();

    virtual void reset();
    virtual void operator+=(**double**);

    int similarSamples(**double**);

    int buckets();

    double bucketThreshold(**int** i);
    int inBucket(**int** i);
    void printBuckets(ostream&);
};

FIGURE 7.1. Interface of the SampleHistogram Class.

□   ≡ local data member

▣   ≡ inherited data member

○   ≡ local member function

◎   ≡ inherited member function

FIGURE 7.2. Notation Used for Derived Enchanced Call Graph.

- Add a row for each newly defined[2] data member of the derived class $D_{derived}$.

---

[2]We use the term *newly-defined* to specify attributes that have been redefined in class $D_{derived}$ as well as those that have been defined in class $D_{derived}$ but are not part of class B_{base}.

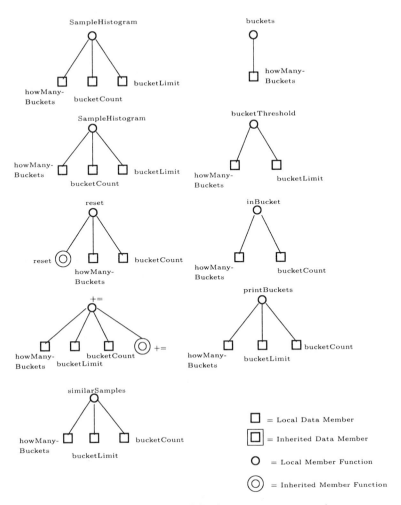

FIGURE 7.3. ECG of `SampleHistogram` class.

- Add a column for each newly defined member function of class $D_{derived}$.

Note that there may be multiple rows/columns with the same name for the redefined data members/member functions respectively.

As shown in figure 7.4, a complete circle around the name of a member function of a derived class denotes that this member function is redefining an existing member function of its base class. Similarly a dotted circle around the name of a member function of a base class indicates that a derived class is redefining this member function.

Here the class under test is `SampleHistogram` and its base class is `SampleStatistic`. The MaDUM of `SampleStatistic` class is shown in figure 6.9 in chapter 6.

SampleHistogram class has three data members and, excluding the destructor, eight member functions. Thus $MaDUM_{SampleHistogram}$ has eight rows. Three of these rows are for its local data members and five are for inherited data members from its base class. Similarly, $MaDUM_{SampleHistogram}$ has twenty columns, eight for local member functions and twelve for inherited ones. $MaDUM_{SampleHistogram}$ is shown in figure 7.4. Notice that it has repeated entries for the redefined methods, *reset* and *+=*.

7.1.3   Fill MaDUM$_{derived}$

The MaDUM of a class $D_{derived}$, with a single base class B_{base}, is shown in figure 7.5. The MaDUM of a derived class can be partitioned into four quadrants.

Quadrant I represents the relationship between member functions of the derived class and the inherited data members from the base class.

If a newly defined member function $m_{derived}$ manipulates a data member of the base class directly, then the appropriate type of data member usage is marked in the corresponding box of the MaDUM.[3] Similarly, if a newly defined member function $m_{derived}$ calls an inherited member function m_{base} of the base class, then the column of m_{base} is unioned with the column of $m_{derived}$ and the result is stored in the column of $m_{derived}$. This means that all data members used by m_{base} are also being used by $m_{derived}$. If we represent a column by $C_{method_{class}}$, then

$$C_{m_{derived}} = C_{m_{derived}} \cup C_{m_{base}}.$$

Redundant entries, to be described later, are removed to ensure that this matrix is minimal.

Quadrant II is the usage relationship between inherited attributes from the base class only. This region will not be altered since it is the same as the MaDUM of class B_{base}. Initially, however, we use the combined DUM of base class that has all the *redundant* entries in it too. This is necessary to cover those cases where a member function of the derived class uses some data member of the base class indirectly. If the same member function also uses the same data member through another branch, then the data member must be retested. However, the entry may have been removed as redundant. The combined DUM of the base class is initially used to cover such cases. Eventually the MaDUM of the base class is used in this quadrant.

Quadrant III is the usage relationship between data members of the derived class and the member functions inherited from the base class. Since a base class has no a priori knowledge about the data members

---

[3]The types of data member usage are the same as those given in section 6.3.2.

	Samp-leStat (reset) (+=)	samples	mean	stdDev	var	min	max	conf. conf.	error	Sampl-eHisto (reset) (+=)	similar-samples	buckets	bucket-Threshold	inBucket	print-Buckets
n															
x															
x2															
minValue															
maxValue															
howManyBuckets															
bucketCount															
bucketLimit															

FIGURE 7.4. DUM for the Derived Class `SampleHistogram`.

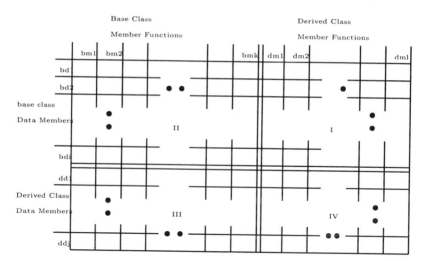

FIGURE 7.5. $DUM_{derived}$ for class $D_{derived}$.

of one of its derived classes, intuitively this quadrant should be empty. This, however, is not true. Consider, for example, the classes given in figure 7.6. Class B is the base class of class C. A method *doSomething()* has been redefined in class C such that it provides a different implementation than the one provided by class B and acts on totally different data members. When a call to method *myJob()* is made on an object of type B, it invokes B's *doSomething()*. However, if the method *myJob()* is invoked on an object of type C, then C's *doSomething()* is called. It has caused a method, *myJob()*, of the base class to act on the data member, c, of one of its derived classes. This is counter intuitive. Even though the base class has no a priori knowledge about the data members of its derived classes, it still acts on them. This must be reflected somewhere in $DUM_{derived}$. Such cases would be described by quadrant III of $DUM_{derived}$.

Such a scenario would arise if a member function $m1_{base}$ calls another member function $m2_{base}$ and the method $m2$ is redefined in one of the derived classes. To update $DUM_{derived}$, a union of $m1_{base}$ and $m2_{derived}$ should be performed, and the results should be stored in $m1_{base}$. Thus, in terms of columns,

$$C_{m1_{base}} = C_{m1_{base}} \cup C_{m2_{derived}}.$$

Quadrant IV is the usage relationship between the local attributes of class $D_{derived}$ only. The entries in this area are marked by looking at only the member functions of class $D_{derived}$. $ECG_{derived}$ is used to mark the entries in this quadrant. The entries are then reduced by using the procedure described in appendix D.

```
class B {
    int b;
  public:
    virtual void myJob() { doSomething(); }
    virtual void doSomething() {b=1;}
    ...
};

class C : public B {
    int c;
  public:
    virtual void doSomething() {c=1;}
};

main() {
    B* bp = new B();
    C* cp = new C();

    bp→myJob(); // calls B's doSomething()

    cp→myJob(); // calls C's doSomething()

}
```

FIGURE 7.6. How to Fill Quadrant III of $DUM_{derived}$: Example Classes

The order in which these quadrants are filled is important. Quadrant II has already been filled using the test history of the base class. Quadrant IV should be filled before the remaining ones since it reflects the local data members usage of a derived class. The information in quadrant IV is needed to fill the entries in quadrant III, which is filled next since some methods of the derived class may be calling methods of the base class and complete information about the methods of the base class will be available only after quadrant III has been filled. Quadrant I should be filled last.

Filling out and reducing the MaDUM of a derived class is more complicated than is the same task for its base class counterpart. Appendix 7.1.2 outlines the complete procedure for drawing a MaDUM of a derived class. The procedure uses a notation by which each attribute may be subscripted by the letter k or the letter s to denote that the attribute belongs to *base* or *subclass*, respectively.

1. Let
   $S = SampleHistogram$
   $K = SampleStatistic$
   $ECG(S) = \langle M(S), D(S), E_{md}, E_{mm}, U_d(K), U_m(K) \rangle,$

where

$$M(S) = \{SampleHistogram, reset, +=, similarSamples, buckets,$$
$$bucketThreshold, inBucket, printBuckets\}$$

$$D(S) = \{howManyBuckets, bucketCount, bucketLimit\}$$

$$
\begin{aligned}
E_{md} = \{&(SampleHistogram, howManyBuckets), \\
&(SampleHistogram, bucketCount), \\
&(SampleHistogram, bucketLimit), (reset, howManyBuckets), \\
&(reset, bucketCount), (+=, howManyBuckets), \\
&(+=, bucketCount), (+=, bucketLimit), \\
&(similarSamples, howManyBuckets), \\
&(similarSamples, bucketCount), \\
&(similarSamples, bucketLimit), (buckets, howManyBuckets), \\
&(bucketThreshold, howManyBuckets), \\
&(bucketThreshold, bucketLimit), \\
&(inBucket, howManyBuckets), (inBucket, bucketCount), \\
&(printBuckets, howManyBuckets), \\
&(printBuckets, bucketCount), \\
&(printBuckets, bucketLimit)\}
\end{aligned}
$$

$$E_{mm} = \{(reset_s, reset_k), (+=_s, +=_k)\}$$

The cardinalities of these sets are then given by

$$U_d(K) = \emptyset$$
$$U_m(K) = \{reset_k, +=_k\}$$
$$n_{mk} = 12$$
$$n_{dk} = 5$$
$$n_{ms} = 8$$
$$n_{ds} = 3$$

2. Fill MaDUM one quadrant at a time.
   $$MaDUM_s = DUM[5+3][12+8]$$

	Sample-Histo-gram	reset	+=	similar-Samples	buckets	bucket-Thresh-old	in-Buckets	print
howMany-Buckets	t_1	o_1	o_1	o_1	r_1	o_1	o_1	o_1
bucketCount	t_1	t_1	t_1	r_1			r_1	o_1
bucketLimit	t_1		o_1	o_1		r_1		o_1

FIGURE 7.7. First-Level DUM for Quadrant IV of SampleHistogram Class.

Fill Quadrant II: The combined DUM of the base class, with *redundant* entries intact, is substituted in quadrant II of the derived class at this stage. The combined DUM of the SampleStatistic class, as shown in figure 6.7, is used at this step.

Fill Quadrant IV: This quadrant describes the relationship between data members and member functions of the SampleHistogram class. We look at the newly defined member functions of the SampleHistogram class and determine which entries to mark. The whole quadrant is filled this way.

$DUM_{IV} = DUM[3][8]$

The DUM for quadrant IV is given in figure 7.7.

Since there is no second-level usage of any data members, there is no DUM for iteration $i = 1$. Hence none of the entries in figure 7.7 are redundant. Thus quadrant IV of the MaDUM of the SampleHistogram class will be the one shown in figure 7.7.

Fill Quadrant III: $MaDUM_{III} = DUM[3][12]$

$M_{ks} = \{reset_s, +=_s\}$

$M_{km} = \emptyset$

Since none of the redefined methods (set M_{ks}) being called by any method of the base class,

$MaDUM_{III} = \emptyset$

Fill Quadrant I: This is the most important quadrant in the data usage matrix $DUM_{SampleHistogram}$. The entries in this quadrant determine the retesting required for the base class SampleStatistic.

$DUM_I = DUM[5][8]$

$U = U_m(K) = \{reset_k, +=_k\}$

For iteration $i = 1$,

$U_{temp} = \{reset_s, +=_s\}$

As mentioned earlier, each method name is subscripted with the key letter k or s to denote its association with the base class or derived class, respectively. Since $reset_s$ invokes $reset_k$, the column of $reset_k$ is repeated in the column of $reset_s$. The same holds for $+=_k$ and $+=_s$. After this operation, quadrant I of the MaDUM looks like the one shown in figure 7.8.

	Sample-Histo-gram	reset	+=	similar-Samples	buckets	bucket-Thresh-old	in-Buckets	print
n		t_2	t_2					
x		t_2	t_2					
x2		t_2	t_2					
minValue		t_2	t_2					
maxValue		t_2	t_2					

FIGURE 7.8. First-Level DUM for Quadrant I of SampleHistogram Class.

Now comparing the columns of $reset_k$ and $reset_s$, we observe that for each data member, the usage type is approximately the same[4]. Hence all the entries in $reset_s$ are redundant. Similarly all the entries in the $+=_s$ column are also redundant. Therefore,
$DUM_I = \emptyset$.

Refill Quadrant II: Finally, combined DUM of Samplestatistic class is replaced by its MaDUM.

Combining DUM's for all quadrants, we obtain the MaDUM for the SampleHistogram class as shown in figure 7.9.

7.1.4   Test Local Attributes

Here we restrict ourselves to the lower half, quadrants III and IV, of $DUM_{derived}$. As mentioned previously, this region describes the usage relationship of the data members of the derived class. Following the test procedure described in chapter 6, methods are categorized into *constructors*, *reporters*, *transformers*, etc., and the testing begins by considering each slice, one at a time.

We do not explain the testing of local attributes of the SampleHistogram class since it is similar to the example given in chapter 6. Suffice to say that the *reporter* method *bucket*, for $slice_{howManyBuckets}$, tested by adding a method in the Tester class. The methods interaction is tested by forming 720 permutations of the remaining seven methods for the howManyBuckets data member. Similarly two reporter methods, *similarSamples* and *inBuckets*, are tested by adding two methods in the Tester class. Interaction of methods is tested by using 24 sequences of the remaining four methods for the $slice_{bucketCount}$. On the same note, a reporter method *bucketThreshold* is tested by adding a method in Tester class. Twenty four sequences are tested for the remaining four methods for the $slice_{bucketLimit}$.

---

[4]Two entries are approximately equal if they differ only in the values of their subscripts.

	SampleStat reset	+=	samples	mean	stdDev	var	min	max	conf.	conf.	error	SampleHisto reset	+=	similar-samples	buckets	bucket-Threshold	inBucket	print-Buckets
n	t	t	r	o	o	o			o	o								
x	t	t		o		o												
x2	t	t				o												
minValue	t	t					r											
maxValue	t	t						r										
howMany-Buckets												t	o	o	r	o	o	o
bucketCount												t	t	r			r	o
bucketLimit												t	o	o		r		o

Category row (perimeter):
SampleStat: c T T R O O O R R O O   SampleHisto: c T T O R O O O

FIGURE 7.9. MaDUM for SampleHistogram Class.

7.1.5   *Retest Inherited Attributes*

More interesting scenarios arise when an inherited data member from a base class B_{base} is being used, directly or indirectly, by a member function of the derived class $D_{derived}$. Since we are testing for the *slices* of a class, if the context of a slice has been modified, then the slice needs to be retested.

The most significant aspect of testing a derived class is to ascertain the inherited attributes that mandate retesting. The inherited attributes and their relationship to newly defined member functions is described by quadrant I of $DUM_{derived}$.

Since quadrant I of the MaDUM for `SampleHistogram` contains no entries, it follows that no retesting is required. For illustration purposes, let us assume that the *redundant* entries for quadrant I are not removed and we have to test for them. The rest of the retesting for inherited attributes is based on this assumption.

Testing of inherited attributes for a class can be divided into two parts: (1) determining the set D_{ir} [5] that warrants retesting and (2) determining test set for each inherited $d_i \in D_{ir}$.

Determining the set D_{ir} is the tougher problem of the two and we shall discuss it at length. Once this set has been finalized, it is easier to find the test set for each member of set D_{ir} using the approach detailed in chapter 6.

Determining the Set D_{ir}

An inherited data member d_i needs to be retested if the number of entries in its row has increased. Thus the set D_{ir} can be given by

$$D_{ir} = \{d_i \mid \sharp(M_{d_i-inh}) > \sharp(M_{d_i-base})\}.$$

Once we have pointed out the inherited attributes that need retesting, the next step is to derive a test set for each element of this set. Since we are into quadrant I of $DUM_{derived}$, let

$$M_{d_i}(D_{derived}) = \{m_i \in M(D_{derived}) \mid m_i @@ d_i\}$$

It can also be given by:

$$M_{d_i}(D_{derived}) = \langle R_{d_i}, \overline{R_{d_i}} \rangle,$$

where

$$R_{d_i} = \{m_i \in M_{d_i}(D_{derived}) \mid m_i \text{ is a } reporter\}$$
$$\overline{R_{d_i}} = M_{d_i}(D_{derived}) - R_{d_i}$$

The number of entries in the row of each inherited data member has increased. Therefore the set D_{ir} for the `SampleHistogram` class is given by

$$D_{ir} = \{n, x, x2, minValue, maxValue\}.$$

The testing of each subset is performed separately.

---

[5] D_{ir} represents the set of data members that are *inherited* and need *retesting*.

Test Reporters A new method is added in the `Tester` class, and the reporter is tested with a series of sequences affecting the data member d_i.

Test Nonreporters All the remaining methods of set $M_{d_i}(D_{derived})$ can then be treated the same. Since we are testing for the interaction of methods, we will only consider the *transformers* and *other*s of d_i from the base class. For most of the cases, including only the *transformer* methods from the base class should be sufficient since it has already been determined that the *other* methods of the base class do not affect the state of the d_i. But for a better coverage of the states of d_i affecting the behavior of methods, *other* methods can also be included.

Let the total set of methods acting on an inherited data member d_i be given by $M'_{d_i}(D_{derived})$. Then

$$M'_{d_i}(D_{derived}) = T_{d_i}(B_{base}) \cup O_{d_i}(B_{base}) \cup \overline{R_{d_i}},$$

where

$$T_{d_i}(B_{base}) = \{m_i \in M_{d_i}(B_{base}) \mid m_i \rightsquigarrow d_i\}.$$

$$O_{d_i}(B_{base}) = \{m_i \in M_{d_i}(B_{base}) \mid m_i \ @@ \ d_i\}.$$

Once the set $M'_{d_i}(D_{derived})$ has been established, we create all possible permutations of this set, such that each method appears in each sequence exactly once, and create the new test set for the data member d_i.

Thus the test set for an inherited data member d_i can be obtained as

$$TS_{d_i}(D_{derived}) = \{TC_{d_i} \mid Seq(TC_{d_i}) \in Perm(M'_{d_i}(D_{derived}))\}.$$

Here it can be argued that some of the base class data members have been left untested, and hence the correctness of a derived class cannot be ascertained. The counter argument is that if a base class data member d_k is not retested, then every possible use of d_k via the derived class member functions can be repeated by using the base class member functions.

We can prove this fact informally. Consider all possible uses of a base class data member in its derived class. For cases where the strategy does not call for retesting this data member, we show that the interaction use of this data member in derived class has been tested in the base class and hence does not require retesting.

Let K and S be base and subclasses, respectively. We continue with the notation where each attribute of a class is subscripted with letters k or s to denote its ownership. Let

$$d_k \in D(K),$$

$$m_{1k}, m_{2k} \in M(K)$$

$$m_{3s}, m_{4s}, m_{5s} \in M(S)$$

Then the possible cases where d_k can be used by a member function of derived class S are as follows:

Case I Direct Usage: If m_{3s} @@ d_k, then there will be an entry in the column of m_{3s} and hence d_k will have to be retested.

Case II Local Indirect Usage: If m_{3s} does not use d_k directly, then if $m_{3s} \longrightarrow^6 m_{4s}$ such that m_{4s} @@ d_k, there will be an entry in the column of m_{4s} and hence d_k will be retested.

Case III Single Inherited Indirect Usage: If $m_{3s} \longrightarrow m_{1k}$ such that m_{1k} @@ d_k, then it is an inherited indirect usage of data member d_k. If m_{3s} does not invoke any other function of base or derived class that directly or indirectly manipulates data member d_k, then

$$DUM[d_k][m_{3s}] = DUM[d_k][m_{1k}].$$

Since this usage of d_k by m_{3s} is essentially the same as the one by m_{1k}, any manipulation of d_k by m_{3s} can also be achieved by invoking m_{1k}. But d_k has already been tested for its possible manipulations by m_{1k}. Hence it does not need retesting and the entry in the column of m_{3s} can be removed.

Case IV Multiple Local Indirect Usage: If

$$m_{3s} \longrightarrow m_{1k} \mid m_{1k} @@ d_k$$

and

$$m_{4s} \longrightarrow m_{2k} \mid m_{2k} @@ d_k,$$

then there are various possibilities.

A: $m_{3s} \longrightarrow m_{4s}$ Here m_{3s} will have two branches through which it uses d_k. Since type of usage or number of usage will differ at m_{3s}, its entry will not be declared *redundant* and hence d_k will need retesting.

B: $m_{4s} \longrightarrow m_{3s}$ Using the same reasoning as for case A, d_k will require retesting.

C: $m_{5s} \longrightarrow m_{3s}$ **and** m_{4s} In this case, there will be a difference in the type or number of usages of d_k at m_{5s}. Hence it cannot be declared *redundant* and thus d_k will require retesting.

D: None of above If both m_{3s} and m_{4s} indirectly use d_k independently, then the entries in both of them will be declared *redundant*. In such a case, if this indirect usage is due to invocation of some member function m_{2k} of the base class, then the effect on the state of d_k can be achieved by invoking m_{2k}. But d_k has already been tested in the base class for both m_{1k} and m_{2k}. This means that entries in both m_{3s} and m_{4s} are *redundant* and hence d_k will not need any retesting.

---

[6]We use $\longrightarrow$ to denote the invocation relationship. Thus A $\longrightarrow$ B implies that a function A invokes a function B.

Let's reconsider the test set for data member n. The test sets for the rest of the data members can be acquired by following the same procedure. First we determine the set $M_n(SampleHistogram)$. As described earlier, this set can be subdivided into two subsets,

$$M_n(D_{derived}) = \langle R_n, \overline{R_n} \rangle.$$

Since $R_n = \emptyset$, therefore

$$\overline{R_n} = \{reset, +=\}.$$

Now we can determine the set of member functions for which data member n needs to be recertified:

$$M'_n(SampleHistogram) = T_n(SampleStatistic) \cup$$
$$O_n(SampleStatistic) \cup$$
$$\overline{R_n}.$$

Here we shall consider only the *transformer* methods from the `SampleStatistic` class since for this case the *other* methods do not affect the state of data member n in any way.

$$M'_n(SampleHistogram) = \{reset_k, +=_k\} \cup \{reset_s, +=_s\}$$

$$M'_n(SampleHistogram) = \{reset_k, +=_k, reset_s, +=_s\}$$

Note that the $reset_k$ and $+=_k$ are for the base class `SampleStatistic` while the other two are for the derived class `SampleHistogram`.

Next the 24 sequences of permutations of these member functions can be created for the set $Perm(M'_n(SampleHistogram))$, and finally the $TS_n(SampleHistogram)$ can be created. The cardinality of this set is 24.

Performing the same procedure for all the inherited data members, we discover that all the inherited data members need the same test sequences. This shows how little retesting is required for the inherited attributes.

We have informally shown, by considering all possible uses of d_k by the member functions of a derived class, that if d_k does not need retesting, then the effect on the state of d_k by the interaction of member functions of derived class can be achieved only through the interaction of member functions of the base class.

7.2 Analysis

We have seen that testing a derived class $D_{derived}$ may require retesting for some of the inherited data members. There are two extreme cases.

Case I: In this case, member functions of a derived class $D_{derived}$ do not use any of the inherited data members. Thus there will be no entry in quadrant I of $DUM_{derived}$. Testing in this case is required only for quadrants III and IV. No testing is required for the inherited data members. The number of test cases needed in this case is given by

$$TS(D_{derived}) = \sum_{i=1}^{num_{d_{derived}}} \sharp(TS_{d_i}(D_{derived})).$$

Case II: All the member functions of the derived class use all the inherited data members. This case requires testing the derived class as a stand-alone class. The test set for D can be given by:

$$TS(D_{derived}) = \sum_{i=1}^{num_{d_{derived}}} \sharp(TS_{d_i}(D_{derived})) + \sum_{j=1}^{num_{d_{base}}} \sharp(TS_{d_j}(B_{base})).$$

As with a lot of other things in life, reality lies between these two extreme cases. Therefore, more information, like the type and number of redefined methods in the derived class, is required before the cardinality of the test set $TS(D_{derived})$ can be determined.

7.3 Summary

Software reuse should not be restricted to code and/or design. Test cases, test scripts, and test data should also be reused for maximum benefit. If the test cases employed for a base class can be reused for its derived classes, then they must be utilized. This has been the theme of the approach presented in this chapter. Testing performed for a base class can be advantageous to the testing of its derived classes. The foremost task in derived class testing is the identification of attributes that mandate retesting as well as those that can safely be used without retesting. We propose a extended test procedure, based on an extended MaDUM, that exploits the relationship between members of base and derived classes to determine the required testing and retesting. Usefulness of the approach is illustrated through a case study.

8

Testing C++ Special Features

C++ is a puissant language. The potency of C++ comes from its vast set of features and its flexibility. For example, it lets a programmer build a new class via the composition of existing or user-defined classes. Some of its other features include various levels of visibility for the attributes of a class, static data members, function pointers, nested classes, generic classes, templates, and so on. This chapter addresses the application of our unit testing approach to such concrete features. Readers who do not use C++ for their object-oriented projects can skip this chapter without any break in continuity.

8.1   Static Data Members

Static data members do not, strictly speaking, constitute the state of the objects of a class[Str91]. All objects of a class that declares a static data member share a single copy of a static data element. Static data members allude the cluttering of global name space[Cop92]. A static data member can be used not only as part of the objects of a class but also without creating any object of that type. This property of static data members mandates a special testing strategy.

A class may have both static data members as well as static member functions. A static member function does not have a this[1] pointer associated with it. Therefore, static member functions can access only the static data members of the class directly. They have to use "." or "→" to access the other data members of the class. They obey the usual access rules for other members of a class[Str91].

Our unit testing approach tests a class one slice at a time. At this time we would like to introduce the concept of a static slice. A static slice is defined as a slice of a class whose data member has been declared static. Static slices may need two types of testing: (1) as part of the class they are declared in and (2)as stand-alone slices. Let us consider each of these cases separately.

Testing Part of a Class: The phrase "part of a class" may be a little misleading since we have already mentioned that a static data member is *not* part of the objects of a class[Str91]. We can say that this type of testing for a static slice is in a given class context.

Let us assume that we have already created a MaDUM of a class and are testing for slices of the class. Let us also assume that the next slice to be tested is a static slice, ss. For a static slice under test, there would be a set of associated, both static and nonstatic, member functions. An ss would be tested just like an ordinary slice except that the constructor of the class cannot initialize the static data member. A static data member has its own stand-alone initializer, and it initializes the data member regardless of the creation of the object of its associated class. The constructor of that class can, however, change this default initialized value. Thus one more column must be added to ss, representing the initialization of the static data member. We can consider it as a special constructor for this data member only. An ss for a given data member s can be given by:

$$ss = < M_s, F_s, I_s >,$$

where
$M_s = \{m_i \mid m_i @@ s$ and m_i is static $\}$
$F_s = \{f_i \mid f_i @@ s$ and f_i is nonstatic $\}$
$I_s = $ definition of s
Testing a static slice then is no different than testing a nonstatic slice.

Testing as Stand-Alone Data Member: A static data member can also be manipulated without creating an object of its associated class. The same holds true for the static member functions of a class. Therefore we need additional testing for static data members of a class. Under these circumstances, a restricted static slice, rss, is created. An rss con-

---

[1]The this is a special pointer that is available only to the member functions. It points to the object for which a member function is called.

sists of a static data member, the static member functions of the class that manipulate the given slice, and its definition. The rss of a static data member s is given by

$$rss = < M_s, I_s >,$$

where M_s and I_s are the same as defined for an ss. The rss is then tested by categorizing the use of the static data member by each of static member functions into *reporter, constructor, transformer,* and *other.*

8.2 Function Pointers

A function pointer can be declared as a data member in a C++ class. The use of function pointers is one way to change the behavior of functions at run time[Cop92]. A function pointer is just like an ordinary pointer except that once initialized, it points to the address of a function. Like any other data member of a class, a function pointer is initializable, modifiable, and reportable. Therefore, we can create a slice for a member function pointer and associate with it all the functions that manipulate it. Each associated member function is marked with appropriate data member use. The pointer to member function is then tested for all possible combinations of *transformer* and *other* methods.

Note, however, that here we are observing only the pointer, not the member function associated with it. Thus only changes to the contents of this function pointer are considered as the transformation to the the state of the object.

8.3 Structs as Data Members

A struct is an aggregate of elements of arbitrary types[Str91]. Like any other data type, a struct can be declared as a data member of a C++ class. In this section, we address the problem of testing C++ classes that contain at least one struct. A struct can be composed of *fundamental* or *derived* types. The elements of a struct can be accessed via "." or "→". If a struct is declared as a data member in a class, then the state of an object of this class type depends on the state of this struct. Any change in the state of the struct affects the state of the object.

For such classes, we suggest a multilevel testing strategy. During the first phase of testing, only the pointer/reference of a struct is tested. There is only one slice of this struct type, and we observe only the changes in its pointer/reference and so on. Once all possible modifications to its address have been verified, the next phase of testing begins. In the second level of testing, a `slice` of a `struct` is expanded into subslices, each of which represents a unique element of the `struct`. The member functions associated with `slice` of `struct` are also associated with the subslices. Each of the subslices is tested individually by our unit testing approach. A tester may have to go to more levels of testing by further subslicing its subslices.

A `struct` may have a pointer to its own `struct` type as its element. For such cases, only the pointer is tested for its manipulation by the member functions of the enclosing class. This pointer is not expanded any further.

One generally observed fact about `structs` is that a member function using one element of a struct uses most of the other elements of the same struct, too[Cra93]. Thus this decomposition of slices should be used only if it reduces the test set for a `struct`. Otherwise the same test set can be used for all elements of a `struct`.

8.4   Nested Classes

A `class` declared within another is called a *nested* class. Nested classes help minimize the number of global names[Str91]. In section 8.3, we resolve the issue of testing classes that have structs as data members. This section can be considered an extension of the previous section. A nested class behaves just like a `struct` except that the nested classes also obey the usual access rules for their data members.

Nested classes can be used from two perspectives: (1) to resolve the naming issue and (2) for containment purposes[Cra93]. If viewed as a naming issue, then a nested class can be tested as a separate class and no special testing is required. However, when used for containment purposes, we propose a multilevel testing strategy. In this case three levels of testing are suggested:

Testing a Pointer/Reference as a Data Member: In this case a `slice` of the nested class data member is considered. The member functions associated with this `slice` are the ones that initialize, report, or transform the pointer/reference to an object of the nested class type. At this level, we consider only the manipulation of the pointer/reference to the nested class object. Our usual technique for testing a fundamental type is used to validate the pointer/reference to the nested class object.

Testing a Nested Class as a Stand-Alone Class: We can apply our testing technique directly by creating an object of type nested class and then applying our testing strategy. There is a small complication here, however. The scope of a nested class is restricted to the enclosing class it is declared in. Hence it is not possible to create an object of the nested class type directly, and the scope resolution operator :: has to be used.

An object of nested class type `Inner` can by created by

$$Enclosed :: Inner\ nestedObject;$$

Testing a Nested Class in the Scope of the Enclosing Class: Here the `slice` for an object of nested class type is considered. The `slice` is then expanded into n subslices, where n is the number of data members of the nested class. Each subslice of the nested class, ssn can be given by a tuple. If E is the enclosing class and N is the nested class, then ssn is given by

$$ssn = \langle d, M_e, M_n \rangle,$$

where
$d =$ data member of subslice ssn,
$M_e = \{m_i \mid m_i \in M(E) \text{ and } m_i\ @@\ d$
$M_e = \{m_j \mid m_j \in M(N) \text{ and } m_j\ @@\ d$
The combined effect of the member functions of both enclosing and nested classes is considered on each of the subslices. A *reporter* method is added to the `Tester` class for each of the data members of the nested class. Each `subslice` is then individually tested to validate the nested class.

8.5   Member Access Control

A `class` can control accessibility of its member to functions other than its own member functions[Cop92]. This is called *horizontal access control*. *Vertical access control* pertains to the access between base classes and derived classes.

Accessibility of a member of a C++ class can be `private, protected,` and `public`:

private: Members declared under this category can be used only by the member functions, member initializers, and friends of the class in which they are declared.

protected: Members under this category have the same access level as `private` members. In addition, they can also be accessed by the member functions and friends of any classes derived from the class in which they are declared.

public: Members declared `public` can be accessed by any function or initializer.

The `private/protected` member functions of a class cannot be used by an external client unless the external client is declared as a `friend` in the same class. This implies that an external client can use only the public interface of a class. Similarly, a derived class can access only the `public` and `protected` interface of a class. But a member function of a class can invoke all other member functions of its own class regardless of their access level. Based on these interface access levels, three levels of testing are clearly visible for a class.

1. **Testing a Class from an Unrelated[2] Client's Perspective:** In this case, only the `public` interface of the class and the data members it manipulates are considered. Since a client can invoke only the `public` interface, interaction of methods is tested only for these member functions.
2. **Testing a Class from Its Derived Class's Perspective:** A derived class can access the `protected` and `public` interfaces of a class. While testing from the perspective of a derived class, member functions declared `protected` and `public` are considered. Similarly, only the data members manipulated by these member functions are tested for.
3. **Testing a Class from Its Own Perspective:** For a class, all its member functions can be invoked by any of its member functions or initializers. Hence all data members and member functions have to be taken into account for this type of testing.

Item 1 is the weakest form of testing while item 3 is the strongest. Also, item 2 seems to cover test cases for item 1 as well, whereas item 3 covers test cases for both item 1 and item 2. The unit testing approach described in chapters 6 and 7 is for item 3. It is our strong recommendation that a class be tested from its own perspective, since it would cover all the other cases. In special cases, however, other, weaker forms of testing maybe considered.

8.6   Composite Classes

A class that is formed by two or more objects is known as a *composite* class[Sem93]. The basic idea of *composite* classes is to build complex objects and operations out of simple ones[DLF93]. The objects that a composite class is constituted of are called *composing* objects.

Testing a composite class is similar to testing nested classes. The only difference is that a nested object cannot be created in isolation. The elements of a composite object, however, can be created as stand-alone objects. We assume that the objects forming a composite object have already been tested as stand-alone classes. This simplifies our work for testing a composite object, so we need two-level testing for a composite class.

Testing a Pointer/Reference: First, a composite object is tested using the approach described in chapter 6. Here the pointers/references of the

---

[2]An *unrelated* client of a class possesses the inheritance or friendship relationships with the class.

composing objects are treated as data members. Second, manipulation of these pointers/references by the member functions of the composite object is considered.

Testing a Composite Class with Composing Classes: This level of testing is needed only if a composite class directly manipulates any data member of its composing class. This implies that a member function of a composite class can change the state of its composing object without invoking any method of the composing object. Testing for this slice of the composing object would then be required. Such a slice, for a data member d of a composite class C and one of the composing classes G, would then be given by

$$slice_d = \langle d, M'(C) \cup M'(G) \rangle,$$

where
$d =$ data member of the *slice*
$M'(C) = \{m_i \mid m_i \in M(C) \ and \ m_i \ @@ \ d\}$
$M'(G) = \{m_j \mid m_j \in M(G) \ and \ m_j \ @@ \ d\}$
Thus, in addition to testing slices of the composite object, slices of composing objects would also need to be tested. This testing is rare, however, due to general design guidelines of not declaring any public data members in a class.

8.7 Abstract Classes

Abstract classes are generally used to support the notion of generality[ES90]. They usually provide the common interface for a variety of their derived classes. No objects of an abstract class are created, although a pointer to an object of this type can be declared[ES90]. An abstract class can generally be recognized due to its possession of one or more *pure virtual* [3] functions[ES90].

Our testing strategy for testing abstract classes is very simple. One can argue that no testing for abstract base classes is needed since no object of their type can be created. We counter this argument by stating that abstract classes should undergo whatever minimal testing is possible, since this may reduce the testing for each of their derived classes.

First, we provide empty implementation for each of the pure virtual functions of an abstract class. Then we follow our base class test procedure, as given in chapter 6. Testing abstract base classes is simpler than a regular base class since all columns representing pure virtual functions are empty. The names of these columns are marked with dotted circles to indicate

---

[3] A *pure virtual* function has no definition and its declaration is appended by the *pure* specifier (= 0)[ES90].

that a derived class is redefining these member functions. A commutation approach for testing abstract classes is given in [Ove94d].

8.8 Summary

C++ is a general-purpose programming language based on the programming language C. It enhances the facilities offered by C through the addition of concepts like classes, inline functions, operator overloading, function name overloading, constant types, references, free store management operators, and function argument checking and type conversion.

The additional concepts put forth by object-oriented technology in general and C++ in particular often pose significant challenges to the testing community. We propose a possible unit testing solution for some of the more intricate features of C++. Being a potent language, C++ has many more raveling features. The general guidelines provided in this chapter should prepare the reader for testing other such features.

9

Code Reviews

There are two primary means of testing any software, *computer-based testing* and *human-based testing*. Computer-based software testing requires automated tools to generate the test cases and subsequently to execute them. Human-based software testing, on the other hand, involves the visual inspection of a software fragment by a team of qualified individuals. While computer-based testing has its merits, human-based testing of software has also been found to detect errors effectively. These techniques are complementary, and both should be used for improving the quality of any software. The prevalence of certain types of errors[Bas93] in object-oriented software also warrants the use of human-based software testing due to the lack of good computer tools to detect these types of errors.

Two basic forms of human-based testing are *code inspections* and *code walk-throughs*. Although there are some dissimilarities between the two approaches, we consider them synonymously for simplicity. The terms *code inspections, code walk-throughs,* and *code reviews* are used interchangeably in the rest of this book.

9.1 Objective

Software reviews are almost as old as the the software itself. It is said that Charles Babbage and von Neumann regularly asked others to examine their programs[WF84]. It is interesting to note that reviews are an important part of many other disciplines, such as financial accounting and building construction. Yet they are still not significant part of software engineering[KM93]. Reviews of large systems have reduced the number of errors reaching the testing phases by a factor of 10[FW82]. Although the benefits of software reviews are obvious, there is still hesitance in accepting them as an integral part of software development.

Code inspection can be defined as[Fag76]

> a set of procedures and error-detection techniques for group code reading.

Code inspection is a technique for making the code consistent, correct, and maintainable. Any nontrivial project is developed by a team of software engineers including programmers, designers, testers, and so on. Normally, programmers take justifiable pride in their individual style of writing code. They must, however subject their creativity to the controlling framework of certain guidelines. Software consistency is an essential attribute of a maintainable software system. According to some estimates, software maintenance consumes approximately 60 percent of the cost of the whole project.

Code inspection aids in the development of decorous code. Another pair of eyes and a different perspective on a solution to a problem can identify errors that would otherwise be invisible to the code's devisor. It has been observed that programmers tend to make more mistakes in correcting an error detected during computer-based testing than in correcting an error found earlier than the testing phase[Mye79]. There are various reasons for this phenomenon, the most compelling of which is that the computer-based testing mostly reveals only the symptoms of an error, not its true cause.

The code review process is a constructive process. Its intent is to improve the quality of software by eliminating as many errors as possible in the earlier stages of development. When a programmer is writing a `class`, a software module, or a software component, the specifications may be unclear and the programmer may make certain assumptions about them. Some of this incertitude can be eliminated by a code review committee[1] that reviews the code to determine that the solution is construing the right problem. The code review committee also determines whether the problem is correctly resolved by walking through each line of the code. Each member of the committee looks at the solution to the problem from his or her own perspective. Any doubts are raised as questions and the programmer is provided useful feedback for either correcting or improving the code. It must be remembered, however, that the objective of code reviews is to detect the errors, *not* to correct them. It is very easy for reviewers to slide down the slippery slope of proposing solutions during a review meeting, but they should take pains to avoid doing so.

---

[1]A team responsible for reviewing certain software code.

Another by-product of code reviews is the educational experience for the whole code review team. A programmer may have developed some neat techniques to resolve a recurring problem. Since certain types of programming problems occur again and again, other member of the team can use the same approach when they run across similar problems. A code review also provides the programmer the opportunity to openly discuss his or her ideas publicly and provide a rationale for them.

9.2 Approach

First and foremost, we have to have faith in code reviews. On many projects are nonbelievers. Only after a few code review meetings and through hard evidence do some of them agree to the benefits of code reviews. Some of nonbelievers may turn a code review meeting into a social gathering. Such behavior must be stopped in its trades as it undermines the effectiveness of code reviews.

There are various types of code reviews, including *Fagan inspections* [Fag76] [Fag86], *code walk-throughs* [FW82], the *cleanroom* approach [Dye87] [SBB87], the *N-fold inspection* method [SMT92], and *phased inspection* [KM93]. Our approach closely resembles *Fagan inspections.*

Due to its significance, a code review should be held in a formal setting. AS proper code review committee should be formed and highly qualified people should be involved. Nonbelievers always object that the development team does not have time for code reviews. But if certain errors are permitted to slip through, the project will be delayed more when the errors are detected later in the process. Code reviews therefore help to keep a project on schedule by detecting and eliminating errors early.

Code review committees can be rotational as well. This ensures that everyone gets a chance to be part of the quality assurance process. It also enhances the educational experience of the code review committee. It may even help a member of a code review committee in identifying errors in his or her own code, even though hi or her own code is not under review. This rotation in committee membership also reduces the time objection of the nonbelievers.

Proper attitude must be established for code reviews. Any feedback during the code review process should not be considered as an attack on the programmer. The code review process is an educational experience, and everyone in the team benefits from it. Code reviews are done purely for consistency, correctness, and high quality of software. Any comments, suggestions, and questions during the code review meetings are to be viewed as constructive to all involved parties. Everyone benefits from supportive code review sessions not only in building better software in gaining an understanding of different and better ways to develop software. It might be easier to develop a nonconfrontational atmosphere if all comments and suggestions are presented as questions.

9.3   Activities

Code inspection and review is one of the oldest and most powerful tools for software quality assurance. Years of experience by researchers in the area suggests the following code review guidelines[FFN91][Buc81].

Code Inspection Meetings Per Day: Experience suggests that for code reviews to be effective, no more than one inspection meeting should be held per person per day. Code inspection is a mentally exhaustive task. If a person is involved in more than one such meeting in a day, he/she can no longer do an effective code review after the first meeting.

Code Inspection Meeting Time: The optimal time for a code review meeting has been determined to be between 90 and 120 minutes. Average human capacity for continuous focus is approximately two hours. If the meeting goes beyond the two-hour limit, people start to lose focus and interest in the proceedings. Therefore, for the most productive code review meetings, they should not last more than two hours.

Code Inspection Rate: Traditionally, code reviews were done at a rate of 100 noncommented lines of code per hour. Because lines of code are a meaningless metric, we propose that only one component or subsystem should be code reviewed in a meeting. In object-oriented development, a problem is solved by a set of interacting objects. A programmer creates new classes or inherits from existing ones to solve a problem. Each code inspection meeting should focus on a single nontrivial problem that the programmer has solved. The code for all the classes for which the programmer creates the objects should be inspected.

Code Inspection Results: The results of code inspection should never be used for evaluations. The objective of code reviews is to improve the quality of a project, not to test individuals. Constructive feedback from code reviews in itself improves the quality of individual programming techniques.

9.3.1   Typical Activities in Code Reviews

A typical order of activities in code reviews is shown in figure 9.1. This set of activities is specific to reviewing software programs. However, these review activities are not limited to a programming language code; they can very well be used for other reviews like design reviews.

Inform Moderator: Developers are responsible for having their code reviewed. A developer is the best judge of the best time for a code review.

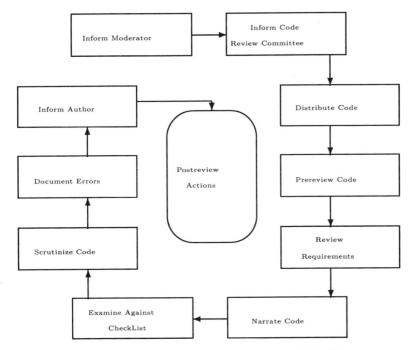

FIGURE 9.1. Typical Activities During Code Review.

The developer sets a time when a portion of a code is to be reviewed and informs a moderator.

Inform Code Review Committee: The moderator informs each member of the code review committee and sets up a code review meeting time and place that is convenient for every member of the team.

Distribute Code: The developer freezes the code and provides electronic and/or hard copies of the source code and design documents to the members of the code review committee. The ideal time to distribute the code is two to three days ahead of the meeting.

Prereview Code: Each member of the code review team is responsible for going through the code before the meeting. Each member should take notes and mark the code with any questions or doubts.

Review Requirements: Each member of the committee is responsible for bringing a hard copy of the source code under review, along with notes and questions. The developer is responsible for bringing the following to the code review meeting.

- A hard copy of the code to be reviewed
- The design documents(object model, interaction diagrams etc.)
- Results of code compilation
- Results of any program checker/verifier tool such as lint, lint++, etc.
- Test data used to test the code

- Test cases and the result of test case execution.
- Documentation for any libraries used in the code

Narrate Code: The code review meeting begins with the developer narrating the logic of the program. The simple act of reading one's own program aloud to an audience has been determined to be an effective error-detection technique[Mye79]. It is interesting to note that the most of errors detected during a code review meeting are detected by its developer.

Examine Against Checklists: The program is analyzed against two checklists of historically common programming errors. One checklist consists of the type of errors that occur in any program regardless of the programming language or the design technique used. The other checklist comprises errors typical in the code that has been written using an object-oriented or object-based programming language. The two checklists are provided in sections 9.7 and 9.8. A statistical approach for the synthesis and improvement of checklists is given in[Che96].

Since object-oriented tehcnology is still not completely mature, relatively little is known about typical errors that programmers make using an object-oriented programming language. The expertise of the code review team becomes very useful in detecting errors that may not be part of a checklist. Error checklists should be updated on the discovery of new types of errors.

Scrutinize Code: Each member of the code review team scrutinizes the code from a professional perspective. For example, the database expert ensures that database queries are correct, logical, nonredundant, and efficient. Similarly, the product assurance person brings a set of representative inputs and expected outputs for the program under review. The team then walks through the code with these inputs to verify that the code is behaving as expected. Any discrepancies are noted, and either the expected results or the code are changed.

Document All Modifications: Any and all accepted errors, comments, and suggestions are properly documented. The moderator assigns one member of the code review committee, also known as *recorder*, the task of documenting the results of the code review meeting. The recorder takes notes of all the issues the suggested changes. Figure 9.2 presents a form for documenting the outcome of code review meetings.

If an error is discovered that is not listed in either of the two error checklists, then the appropriate checklist is updated for future code reviews.

Inform Author: The author of the code is handed the list of suggested changes for appropriate action.

Post-Review Actions: A code rereview meeting is scheduled only if the code review team deems it necessary. Alternatively, it is left to the

Code Review Form

SystemName	SubsystemName	Date	Page Number

Change No.	Unit Name (File/Class)	Line No.	Change Description	Options

Moderator	Author	Recorder

☐ Passed
☐ Passed with Necessary Changes
☐ Need Second Review on Date: __/__/__
☐ Verified by: _____

FIGURE 9.2. Sample Code Review Form.

developer and the moderator to ensure that the suggested modifications are integrated into the code and regression tested.

9.4   Resources

A code review team has many inspection roles. In many cases, one person plays more than one inspection role, but the intent of each role is different and must be kept in mind.

A code review committee should neither be small so that each member of the committee is burdened with too many roles nor so large that most of the meetings are spent in irrelevant discussions. Experience suggests that a code inspection team should consist of three to five members. The inspection roles in a code review committee are as follows.

Author: The developer, or the person who has written the code, is responsible for initiating the code review meeting, distributing the copies of the code, narrating the code during the meeting, and making the suggested changes. Author is responsible for attempting to provide error-free code before a code review meeting is called.

Moderator: The moderator is responsible for setting up the code review meeting, conducting the meeting, and later ensuring that the suggested changes are implemented in the code. The moderator ensures that code review meetings do not go off on a tangent. The moderator must ensure that the team stays focused on code review and not on other surrounding technical issues.

Designer: One of the members of the design team is responsible for ensuring the integrity and consistency of the design is maintained.

Domain Expert: The domain expert watches for correctness of the domain knowledge embedded in the code. The logic of a code may have made certain assumptions about the domain rules. The domain expert provides feedback on these aspects of the code. This person should have an in-depth domain knowledge for the application under development.

Product Assurance Expert: The product assurance person reviews the code from a testability perspective, ensuring that there are enough test cases in the test plan to completely test the code. This expert ensures that the output of the code conforms with the expected output from the test cases in the test plan. Any discrepancies are brought up and discussed in the meeting. The result of this discussion prompts one of the two actions. The developer either changes the code to make it consistent with expected output or corrects expected outcome of the test case.

Programming Language Expert: The programming language expert role brings a checklist of common errors for the programming language and watches for them in the code. The person also watches for any other language-related errors in the code.

Database Expert: The database expert is responsible for ensuring correctness of the database queries in the code and that these queries have been written in an optimal manner. Suggested changes are given to the developer.

Recorder: The recorder records the proceedings of the meeting. Once agreed on, suggested changes are recorded on a form similar to the one given in figure 9.2 and handed to the developer.

All of these roles are not mandatory for a code review meeting, depending on the type of code review. The moderator determines which roles are mandated for a particular code review meeting. For example, if the meeting does concerns a code that is not accessing a database, the presence of a database expert at the code review meeting is not necessary.

9.5 Effort

At the project level, a code review requires significant effort. Management must allocate ample time and resources for code reviews in the project plan. We strongly believe that spending a penny can save a dime. For individuals, however, the effort is not very significant. Expending a few hours now to save hundreds later during maintenance is not significant effort at all. We tend to forget this bigger picture when we are in full-speed code crunching mode. It is, however, the responsibility of senior software engineers and software managers not to ignore this global view.

As mentioned earlier, code review meetings should be limited to two hours. Code review meetings in the middle of the week can be very productive. Code review committee has time to individually inspect the code in the beginning of the week, and the developer has time to make the suggested changes in the later half of the week. All the work is done within the work week without a weekend interruption where some implicit feedback may be lost.

9.6 Acceptance Criteria

The code review committee is the primary judge of whether code is ready to be accepted. When changes are suggested, the developer goes back and makes changes. The code review committee can monitor the changes in one of three ways. They can leave it up to the developer to incorporate the suggested modifications into the code and test them. For minor cosmetic changes, this choice is acceptable but not recommended. More often than not, when a developer is making cosmetic changes in the code, he or she will notice some other "minor" problems with the code and will "correct" them. This can have side effects that the developer may not be aware of.

The second choice is to leave the suggested changes with the developer and have the moderator or another member of code review committee review the modified code. This is a pragmatic solution. It does not involve expenditure of everyone's time, and it validates the modified code against the suggested changes.

The third choice is made in the extreme cases where the code review meeting calls for significant changes in the code. In this case, another code review meeting is scheduled to go over the modified code. This case is less common than the other two.

9.7   Language-Independent Errors Checklist

This checklist is not meant to be exhaustive. Instead it is intended to be representative and illustrative. Many of these errors have been detailed in Myers[Mye79], Frakes et el.[FFN91], Bently[Ben82], Fagan[Fag86], and Freedman and Weinberg[FW82]. A careful reader would note that many of these errors can easily be detected by the smart compilers that are available today. We do not disagree with that. However, we believe that software engineers should be aware of all sorts of possible errors. If engineers know what the errors are, they can consciously attempt to avoid them.

9.7.1   Data Reference Errors

Data reference errors[FFN91][Mye79] arise from misuse of data in a function or in a method of a class. Some typical data reference errors are the following.

- Reference to an uninitialized or incorrectly set variable. An object may have been uninitialized, or point to an unintended object. Similarly, a member of an object may be uninitialized or initialized to an incorrect value.
- Subscripts within bounds. Any reference to an array element should be within the bounds the array.
- Noninteger subscripts. Each subscript of an array must have an integer value. It is sometimes a dangerous practice to use names for the subscripts.
- Dangling references. A reference not pointing to an allocated space in memory is called a *dangling reference*. The life of a reference pointer should not be more than that of the allocated storage.
- Correct aliasing. Aliasing, in general, is error prone. When one has to use it, all intended aliases for a single entity must reference to the same entity.
- Exceeded strings limits. Access to an out-of-bound string element must be avoided.
- Off-by-one errors in indexing or subscripting operations. This is one of the most notorious errors. Since the first element of an array is refer-

enced as the 0th element, it is very easy to incorrectly acc
element while one intended to access the (n-1)th element.
- Defined but unused variables. These variables clutter the nan
the program, and hence can be error-prone during program
during maintenance.

9.7.2 Data Declaration Errors

These errors arise from incorrect use of data types or from incorrectly
initializing or naming data structures. Common examples of such errors
follow.

- Default values of attributes not set. Attributes must be explicitly initialized for their default values. For example, in a certain language, the
default initial value of an *integer* could be zero. The rules of safe programming mandate that at the declaration time of *integer*, it should be
explicitly set to value zero.
- Arrays and strings initialized inappropriately. Similar to initialization
of attributes, array and strings must be explicitly set to default values.
- Incorrect lengths, types, and storage classes assigned. Again, the length,
type, and memory allocation of a data type must be correctly and
explicitly specified at its declaration time.
- Initialization inconsistent with storage class. One must ensure that the
values stored in a variable are of the same type as the variable data
type. For example, it is an error to store *char* in *int*, and vice versa.

9.7.3 Computation Errors

Following are some examples of computation errors.

- Mixed-mode computations. Any mixed-mode computation should be
avoided. An example of such a computation is the addition of an integer
variable to a floating-point variable.
- Target size less than size of assigned value. One must ensure that the
result of a computation is stored in a data type that can handle the
result, and hence does not lose any part of it. For example, storing the
value 25.33 in an integer can lose the numbers after the decimal point.
- Possible division by zero. A divisor in a division operation must never
be zero. In some languages, it can result in unexpected behavior.
- Variable value outside meaningful range. The value of a variable must
be within the range of its intended meaning.
- Operator precedence misunderstood. It is always a good practice to
explicitly specify the order of computation in a complex statement. For
example, if a statement is combines addition and division operations,
the order of computation can be specified using parentheses.

- Integer divisions incorrect. Integer division can produce some unexpected results depending on the values of the operands.

9.7.4 Comparison Errors

Comparison errors occur when variables are incorrectly compared. The following errors are the typical ones.

- Comparison relationships misunderstood. One must ensure that the data types of the operands being compared are the same.
- Boolean expressions incorrect. The meaning of a boolean expression that is combining more than one operators (*and, or, not*) must correctly represent the intention of the statement.
- Comparison and boolean expression mixed incorrectly. It is very common to make mistakes in the boolean expression, especially when program statements are used within a conditional expression.
- Operator precedence misunderstood. For a conditional expression containing more than one boolean expression, and operator, either the precedence order of the computation must be explicitly stated or there should be no doubts about it.
- Compiler evaluation of boolean expression misunderstood. Compilers may evaluate boolean expressions differently. The person writing the code must either understand the compiler's order of evaluation for boolean expressions or explicitly specify the order.

9.7.5 Control Flow Errors

Control errors occur when the thread of control of a program takes an incorrect turn. Some examples of control flow errors follow.

- Unreachable code. Any line of code, any function, any unused variable, and any unused method must not be included in the program.
- Nonterminating loops. Termination of each loop in a program must be validated, at least informally.
- Multiway branches exceeded. For example, each *case* statement must have a **default** branch for all unaccounted conditions in the *case* statement.
- Off-by-one iteration errors. Again, due to to counting beginning at 0, any inadvertent one-too-many or one-too-few errors must be avoided.

9.7.6 Input/Output Errors

This type of error occurs when there is an erroneous input from or output to peripherals. Examples of input/output errors include the following.

- File attributes incorrect. Generally it is not good practice to hard code the attributes of a file (e.g., file name) explicitly declared inside the code. If a scenario so mandates, then these attributes must be correct.
- Files opened/closed before/after use. Each of the files, streams, and buffers must be correctly *opened* and correctly *closed*.
- End-of-file condition handled incorrectly. If a file is accessed, then the end-of-file must be correctly determined.
- File not found. If a program tries to *open* a file and the file is not found, the error must be correctly handled.
- Textual/grammatical/spellings errors in output. Error reporting, information reporting, and other textual messages to the users of a system must be free of spelling and grammatical mistakes.

9.7.7 Interface Errors

Examples of errors due to incorrect interface between objects or modules include the following.

- Order of signature. The order of signature in a call to a method must be consistent with the actual signature. A case is more error prone when the data type of all parameters is the same.
- Type of signature. Each of data type of signature in a call to a method must be consistent with the data types of the method.
- Number of parameters in a signature. Due to the dynamic binding feature of object-oriented technology, a call to a method may be directed to a different method if the number or type of parameters are different.
- Incorrect interfacing to library functions.A call to library methods or functions,must have the correct number and type of parameters in its signature.
- Call by reference and call by value parameters used improperly. If the calling method intends to have the value of one of its parameters changed by the called method, it should be passed by reference. Otherwise, it should be passed by value.

9.7.8 Domain Errors

These errors appear due to misconception about the application domain.

- Domain knowledge misunderstood. Many errors are introduced due to either lack of or misconception about domain knowledge on the part of the designers/developers.

9.7.9 Performance Errors

These errors contribute to the function not executing within acceptable bounds. Some of the examples follow.

- Recomputing a function whose value never changes. Computation should be done only if required. Unnecessary and redundant computations should be avoided.
- Unnecessary logical tests within a loop. During the testing of logical conditions, unnecessary tests should be avoided. For example, if a conditional statement has an *OR* operator between the conditions and one of the conditions has been found to be true, there is no need to compute the second condition.

9.7.10 Other Errors

- Any warning or informational messages. Do not ignore *WARNING* messages issued by the compiler. Sometimes they can lead to serious errors in the program.
- Inputs checked for validity. If a program requires user input, these inputs must be validated. With distributed programming, these checks are more critical to avoid any unnecessary network traffic.
- Incorrect or incomplete comments. Programmers are historically not good at documenting programs. But the same programmers whin about lack of understandability in the programs of others. Comments should be complete, precise, and correct.
- Inconsistent comments within code. Comments at various levels of a program must be consistent with each other.

9.8   Object-Oriented Errors Checklist

This list of errors is specific to the C++ language. Most of these errors, however, are applicable to other object-oriented and object-based languages. Details of these errors can by found in Myers[Mey92][Mey96] and Spuler[Spu94].

- Misuse of Macros. Whenever one writes macros that look like functions, one should be explicit in parenthesizing them. Otherwise, it can lead to confusion due to the many ways a function can be called.
- Allocating memory without handling out-of-memory errors. Whenever one allocates memory, one should consider out-of-memory errors and handle them gracefully.
- Freeing memory without calling destructors. *New* and *delete* are superior choices to allocation and deallocation of memory than *malloc* and *free*.

- Using C-type comments within C-type comments. Usage of C-type comments should be avoided since when comments are inserted within a big block of comments, a comment can inadvertently end.
- Improper deletion of memory allocated to an array of objects. When memory is allocated to an array of objects using *new*, constructors for all of these objects are called. If this memory is deallocated using just *delete* on the array, the destructors may not be properly called. A good rule of thumb is that if the operator [] is used in the *new* call, then the same operator should be used in the *delete* call as well.
- Not freeing the dynamically allocated memory. If a pointer member is added to a `class`, then it must be allocated memory in each of the constructors of the class. Similarly, the same memory must be deallocated in the destructor of the `class`.
- Not deleting the memory. If memory is allocated for any member of the class, it must be deallocated as well.
- Memory deletion of one object by another object. Memory allocated for a member of one object must be deallocated by the same object.
- Assigning values to `const` and reference members. Since `const` and reference members can only be initialized, they must be properly set at declaration time.
- Initializing data members out of order of their declaration. Order of data member intialization is the same in C++ as their order of declaration. Hence, the order of data member initialization must be the same as their order of declaration.
- Making destructors nonvirtual in base classes. Virtual destructors should be declared in a class if and only if that class contains at least one virtual function. A virtual destructor tells the compiler to examine the object being deleted to determine where to start calling destructors.
- Have assignment operator (=) return void. Since C++ allows chains of assignments, the overloading of operator (=) must return a reference to `*this` instead of `void`.
- Not assigning all data members in assignment operator. It is a common mistake to miss some data elements while overloading the assignment operator. The operator (=) must carefully be programmed for completeness. The mistake is even more common when new members are added to a class without changing the assignment operator to reflect the addition.
- Assuming inheritance of assignment operator. The assignment operator of a derived class is responsible for ensuring that the assignment operator of its base class is properly called.
- Illegal argument to an operator (+) : Since a compiler may not perform implicit type conversions on all arguments, one must ensure that arguments to the + are appropriate.
- Assigning `const` to nonconst. It is an error for a `const` to be assigned to a nonconst.

- Passing a derived class object by value to a function taking an object of base class as an argument. When a derived class object is passed *by value* to a function that takes the base class, all special features of the derived class are removed to turn it into a base class. Hence the behavior of the object inside the function will be that of the base class only. The solution to this problem is to pass a derived class object as reference.
- Returning reference to a local variable. This is a dangerous practice since one can expose a local variable to change from outside instead of within the object.
- Potential ambiguity due to standard conversions. While writing code, it is always a good practice to be as precise as possible. C++ provides opportunities for programmers to be ambiguous about function calls with default parameters. Such opportunities should be very carefully avoided.
- Inheriting same data member from two different classes. With multiple inheritance, one can inherit a member with the same name from two branches. Here again, the programmer has to be explicit about which member is intended.
- Assigning array using default assignment operator. One should not rely on the default assignment operator for assignment between Array objects. Instead, one should write one's own to ensure that all elements of an Array object are correctly assigned.
- Returning handles to internal data from const member functions. This opens up an opportunity for the internal data of the const member functions to be mutated and hence defeats the whole purpose of const functions. It must be carefully avoided.
- Declaring all member functions nonvirtual. This practice takes the flexibility of specializing in derived classes away from the programmer. Hence the declaration of virtual member functions should be judiciously decided.
- Declaring all member functions virtual. Declaring all member functions virtual can be problematic. Sometimes one does not want certain member functions to be redefined. In such cases, the member functions should be declared nonvirtual.
- Redefining an inherited nonvirtual function. This can cause objects to behave differently than intented and hence must be avoided.
- Initialization order of base classes. Base classes are are initialized in the order of declaration if one is using multiple inheritance. Any code that depends on the initialization order of base classes should be avoided.

9.9 Summary

Software reviews have reportedly reduced the number of errors reaching the testing stage by a factor of 10. There are several reasons for complementing software testing with code reviews. Some of the reasons are the expense and imperfection of testing. Other reasons are given in the earlier sections of this chapter.

Software reviews are one of the most cost-effective tools the software engineering community has today. The argument is more applicable to the object-oriented software engineering community that has a scarcity of good software testing tools. The potency of a tool, however, is only as good as its user. Belief in the potential benefits, seriousness of effort, and commitment of time and resources are the essential ingredients to the success of code reviews.

10

Integration Testing

Application of traditional software testing techniques to object-oriented software is not seamless. Object-oriented languages create many opportunities for errors. The situation is further complicated by the naive application of theoretical constructs and techniques of traditional software development and testing to object-oriented languages. It is incumbent on the software testing community to discover additional levels of integration testing for object-oriented software.

Integration testing is not a trivial task. Traditional approaches to integration testing include top-down, bottom-up, and sandwich approaches[Bei90] [KGH+95b]. In this chapter, we ventilate different potential levels of integration testing in object-oriented context. Then we propose testing techniques for each level. Our proposed testing solutions are extensions of the class-level unit testing approach presented in chapter 6.

10.1 Objective

Like many other terms, the term *integration testing* has diversified meanings. Our definition of integration testing closely resembles one given by Beizer[Bei90]. Integration testing is testing performed to catch any errors when two or more individually developed components are combined to execute their functionalities. A careful reader will notice that this is different from system testing, which we call *integrated system testing*. Typical errors in integration testing include internal and external interface errors, timing errors, and throughput errors. In integrated system testing, typical errors include[Bei90] operating system call errors, performance errors, partition errors.

Overbeck[Ove94a] identifies three types of integration testing strategies:

1. Execution-based integration testing to reveal erroneous interaction of units by tracing their execution.
2. Value-based integration testing to execute the interaction of units by employing certain values. Boundary value testing and equivalent class partitioning testing strategies fall under in category.
3. Function-based integration testing to validate the functionality of components while they interact.

In object-oriented systems, one can identify the following set of possible integration levels.[1]

- integration of members[2] into a single class
- integration of two or more classes through inheritance
- integration of two or more classes through containment
- integration of two or more classes to form a component
- integration of components into a single application

Some people would argue about integration of members into a single class as a form of integration, but we think otherwise. In object-oriented systems, a `class` rather than a function is the unit of composition. In object-oriented systems, classes are not developed by integrating independently devised functions. Instead, classes and their interfaces are declared at design time. The members of a class and their interaction are tested under our unit testing strategy given in chapter 6.

The second level of integration testing is integration of two or more classes through inheritance. Derivation of a new class from a hierarchy of existing ones is a way of class integration. The testing of such integration is covered in chapter 7.

The objective of this chapter is to cover three other kinds of integration testing: integration through containment, integration of classes to form components, and integration of components to devise an application.

The primary objective of integration testing is to ensure that individually developed units/components correctly interact to achieve the desired functionality of a system. There are three aspects to this problem. First, we want to ensure that we get a working skeleton of the system as early as possible. Second, once the basic skeleton has been created, individual parts of the skeleton are aggregated to ensure that these interface and in-

---

[1] A similar decomposition of integration testing levels is given by[JE94].
[2] Both data members and member functions

teract correctly. Finally, integration testing ensures that all parts interact reasonably well to start integrated-system testing.

10.2 Approach

The emphasis on the functionality of software increases as software reaches the later phases of development life cycle. Integration testing, therefore, should focus on the aggregation of software constituents while maintaining their correct behavior. In traditional software development approaches, integration testing focuses on the correct interfaces between multiple units. For object-oriented system, behavior of each of the combined units has a state associated with it. This associated state of an individual component may impact its behavior. Additionally, the *overloading* and *dynamic binding* features of object-oriented languages compel one to test one-to-many possible invocations of the same interfaces.

Integration testing requires careful planning. Bill Hetzel[Het88] identifies five considerations for integration test planning. Our approach to integration testing of object-oriented software consists of finding answers to these consideration in an object-oriented context. Hetzel's five consideration can be abstracted to the following three basic questions.

1. How many objects should be assembled before integration testing commences?
2. What should the order of integration be?
3. Should there be more than one skeleton for integration?

There is no one-fits-all answer to any of these questions. They can be addressed only in a project's context. However, we propose a general solution that works for most object-oriented projects and can be tailored for a specific project.

Integration testing begins as soon as one class is inherited from another. As mentioned earlier, this is one form of integration and integration of these two classes must be taken into account. The approach to this level of integration is proposed in chapter 7.

Our integration testing approach is influenced by the one proposed by Shlaer and Mellor[SM94b]. To understand the this approach, consider a *virtual integration engine* that is responsible for integrating the individual components of a system. This engine has two inputs, a list of *use cases*, and a list of objects. The engine begins by picking the first use case from the list[3]. The integration engine then tries to execute the use-case. When a new object is needed for the use case execution, the object is picked from the list of objects. The selected object is tested with the objects

---

[3]The order of use cases in the list is important and is discussed later.

already picked by the integration engine, for both functionality and correct aggregation. The details of this functionality and aggregation testing are given in section 10.3. The approach is simple and answers the three basic questions about integration testing.

First, the approach specifies that integration testing begins as soon as more than one object is aggregated. It also specifies that order of integration should be per-need basis. Finally, the integration engine provides a skeleton for the integration of objects. A single integration framework is usually ample for modest-size projects. With the increased productivity demands and expectations from object-oriented systems, it is more pragmatic to have a single integration framework.

10.3 Activities

The complete set of activities and the order of integration inherently depends on an individual project. The choices must be made in the context of a project by examining the pros and cons of each option. Such analysis is the key to a good integration testing plan.

In this section, we present two sets of activities. The first set, discussed in section 10.3.1, concentrates on the structure of an application by considering integration of two classes through containment relationship. The second set focuses on the behavior and order of integration for a given set of classes. It is detailed in section 10.3.2.

10.3.1 Structural Integration Testing

Bjarne Stroustrup[Str91] points out that classes do not exist in isolation. Rather they collaborate with other classes to perform meaningful tasks. This collection of collaborating classes may be called a *component*. This section focuses on this structural combination of classes.

There are various possible means through which classes can collaborate with each other. The scope of a collaborating class may be at a method level or a class level. Method-level scope implies that an instance of the collaborating class is either *constructed* or passed as a parameter in a method of the collaborative class. An appropriate call is then made to the collaborating class. Finally, that instance may be *destructed*, if *constructed* within the method, before the end of the method. Class-level collaboration, on the other hand, implies that an instance of a collaborating class is declared as an attribute of a collaborative class, hence a *containment* relationship. There are various possibilities for the two basic forms of collaborations. For example, some people might argue that *private inheritance* is one form of collaboration. We, however, stay away from these discussions. We present

```
class B;

class A {
  public:
    A();
    void A_m1() {bp->B_m1();}
    void A_m2() {bp->B_m2();}
    void A_m3() {bp->B_m2();}
    void A_m4() {bp->B_m3();}
    void A_m4() {...;}
    ~A();

  private:
    B *bp;
};
```

FIGURE 10.1. Integration of Classes A and B through *containment*.

an approach that provides a means for testing two collaborating classes regardless of their collaboration technique.

Typical Set of Activities

Let's assume two classes A and B such that class B is contained[4] within class A. Let's also assume that the relationship between the methods of classes A and B is as shown in Figure 10.1. We propose the following integration testing procedure between the two collaborating classes.

Draw Data Usage Matrix (DUM) of Container Class: The first step in the integration testing of two collaborating classes is to draw the data member usage matrix, as given on page 56. For class A, we draw the DUM along the X-Y axis. The DUM of class A is given in figure 10.2. The only difference between the two DUMs is that the name of the data members of class A are written on the right side in figure 10.2.

Add DUM Of Contained Class: The data usage matrix of the contained class B is then drawn along the Y-Z axis. As we will see, we employ only the member functions relationship between classes A and B. Since we have the DUM of class B from its unit testing anyway, we *paste* the DUM along the Y-Z axis. The DUMs of classes A and B are shown in figure 10.3.

Draw Collaboration Matrix: Next, we draw the intermethod relationship between classes A and B along the X-Z axis. This is accomplished

---

[4]Although we use a containment relationship here, the approach is equally valid for any collaboration relationship.

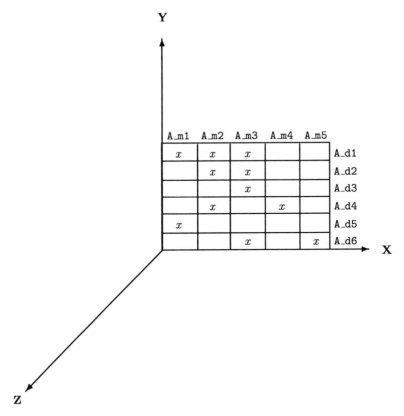

FIGURE 10.2. Data Usage Matrix (DUM) of the Container Class A.

via extending the method columns of class A and class B along the Z axis and X axis, respectively. The matrix along X-Z axis is an $i \star j$ matrix, where i and j are the number of methods in the contained class B and the container class A, respectively. If a method of class A calls a method of class B, then an x is marked in the intersection box of the two methods. This so-called collaboration matrix is shown in figure 10.4.

Determine Test Case for Each Slice: Our testing approach is based on the slices[5] of a class. As shown in chapter 6, we test the sequence of methods for a slice of a class. Let us reuse the test cases used for unit testing container class A. For slice of data member A_d1, let's assume that the test cases are given as follows:

A_m1 A_m2 A_m3
A_m1 A_m3 A_m2
A_m2 A_m1 A_m3

---

[5]See page 52 for the definition of a slice.

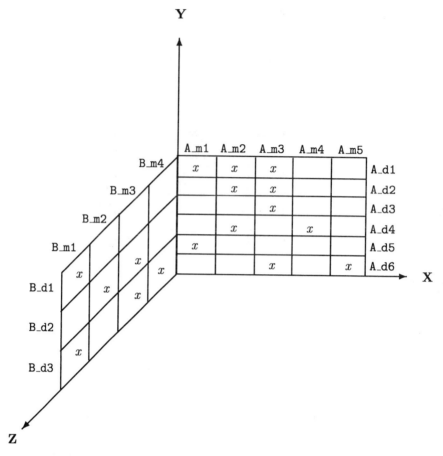

FIGURE 10.3. Data Usage Matrix (DUM) of the Contained Class B with the Container Class A.

A_m2 A_m3 A_m1
A_m3 A_m1 A_m2
A_m3 A_m2 A_m1

Let us assume that all three methods, A_m1, A_m2, and A_m3, can potentially transform the state of data member A_d1.

Extend Sequence of Methods for Both Classes: In this step, we extend the sequence of methods of class A to determine the impact of methods of class B on the data member under test. We extend the sequence of methods that were used to test the slice for A_d1 so that if a member function of the container class calls one or more member functions of the contained class, then it is written within braces. For example, if A_m1 calls B_m1, then each occurrence of A_m1 is replaced

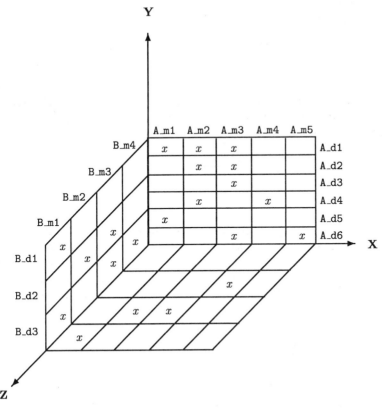

FIGURE 10.4. Data Usage Matrix (DUM) of the Collaborating Classes A and B.

by A_m1(B_m1). Continuing in a similar fashion, the test cases of A_d1 can be rewritten as follows:

A_m1(B_m1) A_m2(B_m2) A_m3(B_m3)
A_m1(B_m1) A_m3(B_m3) A_m2(B_m2)
A_m2(B_m2) A_m1(B_m1) A_m3(B_m3)
A_m2(B_m2) A_m3(B_m3) A_m1(B_m1)
A_m3(B_m3) A_m1(B_m1) A_m2(B_m2)
A_m3(B_m3) A_m2(B_m2) A_m1(B_m1)

Extract Sequence of Methods for Contained Class: Next, we look only at the sequence of methods of contained class that may modify the state of the data member in question, A_d1. By ignoring the methods of the container class, we conclude that the following methods are the potential test cases for slice of A_d1.

B_m1 B_m2 B_m2
B_m1 B_m2 B_m2

B_m2 B_m1 B_m2
B_m2 B_m2 B_m1
B_m2 B_m1 B_m2
B_m2 B_m2 B_m1

Ignore Redundant Sequences: In this step we remove the redundant
sequences in our concluded set of test cases. After eliminating the
unnecessary test cases, we are left with the following set of test cases:

B_m1 B_m2 B_m2
B_m2 B_m1 B_m2
B_m2 B_m2 B_m1

Determine Remaining Sequence of Methods for Container Class:
Next, we replace each call to the contained class method by the method
of the corresponding container class. For example, if B_m1 was called
by A_m1, then each occurrence of B_m1 is replaced by A_m1. Thus our
test cases for the `slice` of A_d1 are reduced to the following sequences.

A_m1 A_m2 A_m3
A_m2 A_m1 A_m3
A_m2 A_m3 A_m1

Execute Test Cases: This is our set of test cases for testing the impact
of a collaborating (contained) class on the `slice` of data member A_d1.
We test A_d1 for this set of test cases the same way we unit tested class
A.

10.3.2   Functional Integration Testing

A fundamental question during integration testing is about the order of
object integration. There are various possible orders of integration. In this
section, we propose a simple order of integration that requires minimal stub
generation. Our integration strategy consists of a virtual integration engine.
There are two queues going into this integration engine. One queue contains
the use cases associated with the project or application. The other queue
contains the usable objects. The virtual engine can be built, or a person can
play the *system integrator* role. The order of integration of objects depends
on the order of use cases. We propose the following set of activities for such
an integration.

Typical Set of Activities

A virtual integration engine and its associated queues are shown in
figure 10.5.

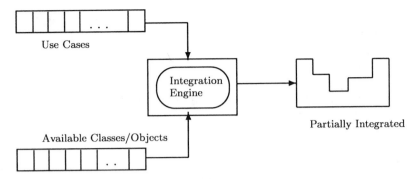

FIGURE 10.5. A Virtual Integration Engine for objects integration.

Order Use-Cases: The first step in our integration strategy is to correctly order the use cases. Various choices are available. Our recommendation is to sort use cases in order of simplicity and interdependence. The use cases that are independent of other use cases should be on the top of the queue. A pseudo-algorithm for ordering use cases would be as follows.

1. Draw a tree of use cases such that the nodes represent the use cases and the edges represent the dependency between use cases.
2. Draw an edge from use case A to use case B, if B is dependent on A. A use case is dependent on another use case if the dependent use case requires some objects from the other use case.
3. Mark all the leaf use cases in the tree. These represent the use cases that no other use cases are dependent on. These use cases should be tested first.
4. Order the leaf use cases in terms of simplicity, which could be in terms of number of classes, aggregate complexity of the classes, and/or interclass dependency.
5. Put the simplest leaf use case at the head of the queue followed by other use cases such that complexity of a use case is higher than the preceding use case and is lower than its proceeding use case.
6. Once all leaf use cases have been ordered, consider the use cases that are dependent on the leaf use cases only. Order this set of use cases in terms of their complexity and put them in the use case queue.
7. Follow the same sequence until all use cases have been ordered in the queue.

Take Next Use Case: Take the next use case in the queue. All required objects for this use case are integrated first.

Get Required Object: Follow the steps of the use case. If an object is required to complete the step, pick the required class from the pool and instantiate it.

Test with Existing Objects: Integrate the new object with the existing objects in the partially integrated system. If the new object collaborates with the existing objects in any way, test the collaboration by employing the procedure outlined in section 10.3.1.

Test Possible Functionality: If all the required objects are in the partially integrated system, test the possible functionality of these objects to ensure that the objects are collaborating according to the functional specifications.

Test Other Requirements: If the partially integrated system conforms to the functional specifications, stress test it for the required load and performance. If the partial system does not satisfy either of the load, performance, or resource requirements, it must be brought to the attention of the development team.

Loop Through: Once satisfied with the integration of the last object, pick the next required object from the pool of objects. If no more objects are required for this use case, select the next use case from the use case queue and repeat the procedure.

An important question arises at this point. What happens if an error is encountered during integration testing? Should we stop the integration testing? How are the errors fixed and brought back to the integration testing environment?

Answers to these questions are simple. Do not stop the integration testing as long as there are use cases in the queue. If an error is encountered during the integration of objects for use case U1, then put U1 at the end of the use case queue. Also, all the nonintegrated use cases in the branch of U1, in the use case tree drawn earlier on page 123, are moved to the end of use case tree. This implies that all use cases dependent upon U1 cannot be integrated until U1 is ready for integration. Similarly, all potentially incorrect classes are removed from the class queue. Potentially incorrect classes are those whose integration has led to the symptoms of an error. At this point, it is hard to say which class the error is in. The integration team should not even try to debug the code. The focus of integration testing is to report the symptom of an error, not to identify the source of an error. File an SPR[6] (Software Problem Report). The error is reported to the development team, and the team fixes the problem. Once the fixed components have been provided by the development team, U1 and its dependent use cases can be upgraded to the front of the queue. The classes removed earlier from the class queue are put back into the queue and are available for integration testing again.

---

[6]Or follow the correct procedure for your organization. This book is about testing, and we refrain from commenting on individual processes and procedures.

10.4   Resources

The most significant integration testing resource is a system integrator. Each project should have at least one person in this role. In case of tools unavailability, this person acts as the integration engine and performs the required integration testing between collaborating objects.

The personnel resources and their roles required for integration testing are described in the following paragraphs. For small to medium-size projects, one person may be adequate for a role. As project size grows, a team may be necessary.

Software Integrator: The prime responsibility of this person is to assemble individually developed components into a system according to its requirements. For small projects, the task can be done without the aid of automated tools. As a project grows in size, the need for automated tools escalates. In case of tools unavailability, this person may act as the integration engine and may have to perform the integration manually.

The software integrator also arranges for any code reviews required for a particular subsystem. The details of code reviews are given in chapter 9. This person is also responsible for getting a team of people together for testing of the use cases during functional integration testing.

Domain Expert: The person is also needed during the functional integration testing subphase. A domain expert should be present to validate the functional requirements of a use case. Correct functionality of a use case provides additional confidence in the integration activity. This person ensures that the partially integrated system can correctly execute some functionality of the desired system.

Database Expert: This person is required for systems that involve persistent storage in either a relational or an object-oriented database. The database expert ensures that all access, queries, and modifications to the data are correctly handled by the partially completed system. This person, like the domain expert, is mainly needed during the functional integration testing.

Product Assurance Expert: A product (or quality) assurance person should be part of any software development activity. During integration testing, this person ensures that the partially completed software conforms to its requirements. During structural integration testing, this person assists the system integrator in determining the integrity of the software.

Senior Developer: A senior member of the design and/or development team should be present during the structural and functional integration testing activities. The developer is responsible for the development aspect of various components and subsystems. This person must have a broad picture of software architecture and be very familiar with the interfaces and structure of individual components. For small projects, the role can very well be played by the system integrator.

Integration Environment: An environment separate from the development environment must be created for software integration testing. The specific needs for this environment are highly project dependent. A separate server is recommended for a client server environment. Appropriate firewalls must be in place for web-based projects. Similarly, client machines must be available to test concurrent use of the software. A separate database instance may be required if the software is database dependent. Most importantly, the environment should be configured as close to the production environment as possible. This would prevent any surprises during integrated-system testing.

10.5   Effort

Integration runs throughout the life time of an object-oriented project. Classes are continuously integrated through inheritance, containment, collaboration, or otherwise. The collaborating classes can either be locally created or be provided by a third-party vendor. In either case, once they are integrated with the home-grown classes, the burden of testing falls on the person responsible for integrating these independently developed classes. The integrated classes are then integrated into components and subsystems. The subsystems are finally bundled together to form meaningful applications.

The reuse potential of these individually developed classes, components, subsystems and/or applications dictates that significant effort be spent in integration testing of these components. Some of the components have been developed with a specific purpose in mind. Extending the components for unintended use provides a perfect opportunity for errors to creep into the resulting software. Hence the integration testing effort is inversely proportional to the amount of reuse. Higher reuse warrants higher integration testing effort.

10.6   Acceptance Criteria

First, a word of caution. If you or your organization are encountering difficulties during integration testing, it can usually be traced to two sources[Het88]. Either unit testing was poorly executed and/or there is no formalism in the integration testing approach. Integration testing, like other testing activities, must be planned and executed properly. Informality and lack of rigor on integration testing by an organization puts the project at a very high risk of failure either during or even before it goes into production.

We cannot emphasize enough the importance of integration testing. Object-oriented projects warrant continuous integration. The need for correct integration increases exponentially as it is done at many levels, and each level demands a different type of testing. A software system is ready for system testing once all individually developed components have been correctly integrated. The correct integration implies that the components have been both structurally and functionally tested, and conform to the requirements. All use cases and requirements must have been met before system testing proceeds.

10.7 Summary

Object-oriented software development is an evolutionary process, and hence the opportunities for integration are abundant. Conceptually, classes are encapsulations of data attributes and their associated functions. Software components are conglomerations of logically and/or physically related classes. A complete software system is also an aggregation of software components. All of these various integration levels warrant contemporary integration techniques. Traditional integration techniques no longer suffice. Integration strategies are needed at class level, component level, subsystem level, and system level. Classes require integration of methods. Various types of class interaction mechanisms demand different testing strategies. Integration of classes into components have their own integration requirements. System integration demands different types of integration testing strategies.

This chapter discusses the various integration levels in object-oriented software development. Integration testing of each level is suggested. An integration testing framework for integrating classes into a system is also proposed.

11

Integrated-System Testing

Integrated-System Testing[1] is an immense and squirrelly task, and it engrosses a major phase of the software development life cycle. Traditionally, all testing activities of a system are intensely sustained during this phase. A significant amount of effort has been invested in the literature[Inc97][Mus96] on the issues related to the system testing. With the advent of *parallel testing life cycle*[Bas99],[2] the unswerving activities of this phase have been distributed throughout the software development life cycle, especially in the object-oriented software development model. In addition to identifying errors at earlier stages, the distribution of testing also reduces the marathon effort required in a single stage.

This chapter addresses object-oriented system testing issues. It provides a set of guidelines and procedures for object-oriented systems. The general principles, however, are applicable to nonobject-oriented systems. The chapter covers both integrated-system and acceptance testing.

An object-oriented software system differs from a procedural one in a major aspect. An object-oriented software system can be considered as a single object. This object, call it `system object`, has a state associated with it. Just like a C++ object, the behavior of a `system object` is contingent upon its initial state. This implies that after performing a particular service, the `system object` may be left in a state contradictory to what was expected. Hence, the initial and final states of the `system object` become

---

[1]system testing, for short.

[2]See figure 2.3 on page 15.

eloquent during system testing. The state of a `system object` is the aggregate state of its inherent constituents. How and when this state should be identified is one of the topics of this chapter. Other aspects of system testing, including *sanity testing, documentation testing, performance testing, stress testing,* and *boundary testing* are also addressed.

11.1   Objective

System testing is a broad term. It is a type of testing exercised during the last stages of software development. Various flavors of system testing include integrated-system testing, alpha testing, beta testing, user-acceptance testing, and so on. We use the term *system testing* to include both integrated-system testing and acceptance testing. Depending on an organization and/or a project, alpha, beta, or any other form of testing may be complemented with this testing approach.

The objective of system software testing is to determine whether the software system is ready for its intended users by observing its behavior, over a period of time, in a simulated or real environment[CHK+95]. System testing tests the completely integrated system for conformance to requirements. It is of paramount importance that all required components have been satisfactorily tested and integrated before the system testing can proceed. It is assumed that all individual components work correctly as stand-alone units.

The tests conducted during system testing must exercise all the functional, performance, stress, and resource requirements of a system. Many functionally correct systems fail miserably during performance or stress testing. Similarly, some systems fail to work in a real environment because the machine resources of the development environment are not available in the development environment. Some systems may perform satisfactorily for a handful of users, but fail for a large number of users. Complete and satisfactory testing of all these aspects, among many others, is the objective of system testing.

Consider, for example, a transaction-processing system. Let us assume that incoming transactions are input into the system through flat files.[3] Let us further assume that there is an `UnProcessedTransactionList` object in the system. This object contains the unprocessed transactions from a single file. If the design mandates that the `UnProcessedTransactionList` object be empty after every file has been successfully processed, then the state of this object must be checked after functional testing of transactions processing. Here the abstract methods that check the *emptiness* of the object suffice to check its abstract state. If this state checking is not performed,

---

[3]ASCII files.

transactions from previous files may be processed repeatedly. Notice that strictly in terms of functionality, all the transactions from a new file will be successfully processed. However, system resources are clearly wasted in processing transactions over and over. This bug will eventually be exposed when the system resources are unable to support the size of the `UnProcessedTransactionList` object.

11.2   Approach

The inherently large and complex task[Het88] of system testing warrants meticulous planning and control. It tends to consume a fair share of resources. The benefits of a *parallel testing model* are clearly visible here. If adequate work is not done at the earlier stages of the software development, the high complexity of this stage is likely to leave many undetected bugs in the system. The use of *parallel testing model* not only promises to catch bugs in the early stages but also distributes the testing work load throughout the development life cycle. This reduces the complexity of work during the system testing stage and provides an conducive environment for effective testing.

The ideal approach during this stage is to scrutinize the system under test for all possible combinations of data under all possible conditions. Unfortunately, this is infeasible in terms of both time and resources. The first step in resolving the dilemma is to cover all requirements; the objective of system testing is to ensure that all types of system requirements are exercised to ascertain their conformity. Second step is to judiciously select test data that cover a broad range of usages. The second step employs significant data values to test the requirements in the first step. Significant data values may include valid values, invalid values, boundary values and so on.

The software engineering community has invested many years in structured software engineering, and there is a lot to be gathered and reused from this experience. Our approach to system testing employs many of the structured software development techniques. We bestow various traditional, and proven, software testing techniques since they are still applicable. We enhance these principles wherever the nature of object-oriented software so demands. For example, during functional testing, we consider the initial and final states of the system. We want to execute the same test under different initial states of the system to observe all possible behaviors of the system.

Determining the state of a system can be an inordinate task. For system testing we are interested only in the *abstract* state of the objects. The *abstract* state of an object is domain-based instead of value-based. For a `IntQueue` object, for example, the *abstract* state determines whether the

`IntQueue` object is *full* or *empty*. In contrast, the *detailed*, or value-based, state of the same object would give us the exact value of each of its data members. The detailed state of an object should already have been checked during unit and integration testing. During system testing, it is not feasible nor should it be necessary to inspect the detailed state of all the objects in a system.[4] System testing requires, however, that after executing a certain functionality, the abstract state of all the involved objects be determined as well.

11.3 Activities

System testing is not restricted to code testing. There are various dimensions to system testing. A software system is composed of many artifacts including programs, documentation (many kinds), and data. Each of these constituents must satisfy its outlined requirements before system testing can conclude.

In this section we identify the constituents of system testing. Each testing activity can be performed by various techniques. We do not recommend specific technique(s) for each type of testing. We do, however, identify the required system testing whose outcome may determine the fitness of its use. Readers interested in specific techniques are referred to[Bei90]. The following sections represent various system testing categories. These activities do not have to be conducted in the order given here. Instead, depending on a project's needs and the testing resources available, many of these activities can be conducted concurrently.

We assume the existence of a prepared and tested test environment before system testing is commenced. The test environment should mimic the eventual production environment as closely as possible. It is a fairly common observation that a system working fine in the development and test environments fails to meet the same expectations in a production environment. To avoid such pitfalls, the testing environment must closely resemble the production environment.

11.3.1 Sanity Testing

Installation and system startup/stop tests (also known as Sanity tests) ensure a smooth installation process and system startup when a software system is initially installed and brought on-line. Once in operation, the system needs to provide capability to the operations staff for logging system

---

[4]An analogy can be drawn with executing a test case for all possible data values. Input data can be partitioned into domains. Representative data is then selected from each of these domains.

activities. All potential operational system failures, e.g., crash recovery testing, is also performed during this phase. Some of the key elements during sanity testing include the following.

System Start-Up Tests: The first step during sanity testing is to ensure that the system can successfully be deployed in its test environment. A system is delivered to the test environment either in the form of a set of executables or in the form of source code. If the source code is provided, the system has to be compiled from the source code. If the system executables are provided, these executables have to be brought up in the test environment. For heterogeneous distributed environments[Mag96], this step warrants extra caution. Based on the deployment architecture, certain objects have to be deployed on different nodes in a distributed environment. Here it must be ensured that all objects are initialized and deployed successfully on the intended nodes. It should also be ensured that these startup objects have ample system resources for their initialization and subsequent operation.

System Stoppage Tests: If the system was successfully started, it is imperative that it can be gracefully shut down. The system should be commanded to shut down by the means provided by the system. Here one has to watch out for any unfreed resources, dangling objects, zombie processes, and so on. The objective of this exercise is to ensure that any resources held by the system are correctly freed up whenever instructed.

System Restart Tests: If the system can successfully be shut down, it should be started and stopped the several times by varying the amount of available system resources. It should also be started by allowing minimum resources dictated by the system documentation.

Operations Manual Tests: The system is started and stopped by following the instructions provided in the operations' manual for the tester. Any missing or ambiguous steps are red-inked in the operations manual.

Fail-Over/Recovery Tests: It is quite realistic to assume that the system under test will unexpectedly go down, at least partially, at some time during its operations. The recovery capabilities of the system are tested by bringing down various processes. If the system provides fail-over capabilities, the backup processes should either be started up or be activated. Identify any discrepancies between the expected and actual recovery behaviors.

11.3.2 Functional Testing

The functionality of the system is checked against its requirements during this activity of system testing. The testing team is responsible for ensuring that each requirement is completely satisfied by the system. Similarly, the testing team must determine that the system satisfies all requirements. Strict black-box testing techniques are generally used for testing the functionality of a system. One of the many possible ways of system functional testing is described here.

Sections 11.3.2 through 11.3.5 assume that the use case tree described on page 123 is available. We can select a use case from the use case tree and run it through various testing types described in sections 11.3.2, 11.3.3, 11.3.4, and 11.3.5. We recommend that the system be tested by selecting simple use cases first, i.e., the leaf use cases in a use case tree. Use cases do not have to be tested sequentially. Contingent on system and testing team resources, testing of many use cases can commence simultaneously. As a matter of fact, it is recommended that, if resources permit, the testing team be divided into smaller groups, each assigned to a set of use cases, its associated requirements and test cases. Concurrent testing creates a more realistic production environment, as well as saves testing time.

The key to effective functional testing is systematic requirements coverageand validation. There are various possibilities for systematic coverage, e.g, functional coverage matrix, requirements validation matrix, transaction flows, and functional boundaries[Het88]. We prefer the requirements validation matrix. A typical example of requirements validation matrix is given in table 11.1. This table is similar to the requirements testing matrix in table 4.1. The essential difference between the two tables is the reference point. Table 4.1 is used for each requirement as specified by the user. In table 11.1, we identify the use case first and then the requirements covered by this use case.

The following is a typical set of activities for functional testing.

Identify the Use-Case: The first step is to identify a use case to be tested. Start with the simplest use cases. Simple use cases are usually toward the leaves of a use case tree.

Select a Primary Course: Execute the *primary* course of the selected use case. A *primary* or *basic course* use case describes the normal course of events for a certain usage of the given system.

Execute a Primary Course: Execute the *primary* course of the selected use case with different valid input values, always starting the system in the same state. The important point here is to test the behavior of the system for a range of input values in a certain stable state of the system. At the end of each test case execution, check the response of the system against the expected response. The expected response of

Use Case	Requirements	Test Cases	Included in System Ver.	Validated

TABLE 11.1. Typical Use Case-Based Requirements Matrix.

the system includes the output values generated by the system, any external entities created by the system (e.g., files), and the final state of the system. The initial and final states of the system are an important addition to the traditional test cases, and is shown in figure 11.1. As mentioned earlier, the initial and final state of the system under test are important as they may determine system response for the next external event.

It is worth remembering that we are not testing the state of every object in the system. For every use case, there is always a set of objects that would actively participate during the execution of a use case. We call these objects the **participant** objects. We are only interested in the initial and final abstract state of the **participant** objects. Testing the detailed state of every object in the system is not a pragmatic solution, and we do not recommend it even in the presence of automated testing tools.

Vary System Initial State: Execute the primary use case by keeping the input values the same but varying the system initial state. This set of test cases checks the behavior of the system under various input states.

Vary Input Values: Repeat the previous step for various input values. Keep the same set of input values for a given test case. Now vary the input values for all the initial states of the system as described in the previous step, and then check the system behavior.

Supply Invalid Input Values: Once satisfied with the system behavior for various input values under different initial states, the next step is to test the system for invalid input values. First vary the invalid input values and keep the same initial state. Then retest the system by varying the initial state of the system while keeping the same input values.

Repeat for Use Case Secondary Course(s): Execute the *secondary* course of the use case. A *secondary* or *alternate course* use case constitutes all sequences other than the *primary* use case. Secondary use cases usually include fault-handling sequences of events. The secondary use case(s) should be tested in a similar fashion to the primary use case.

Loop Through: Go back to the first step and select the next use case to be tested.

11.3.3 Human Factors Testing

A system may or may not include a user interface (UI). If it does, this UI may be graphical, character based, or otherwise. Regardless of its type, if a system includes a UI, it must be thoroughly tested.[5] Part of the system has a human interface. It is important that this part be tested not only

---

[5]See Kepple[Kep94] to find out how GUIs affect test automation.

Test Case Form

TestCase Number: ....

TestCase Name: ....

TestCase Desc: ....

Requirements Traceability

Business Reqmnt: ....

System Reqmnt: ....

Software Reqmnt: ....

Test Case Instructions

Input: ....

System I/P State: ....

Output: ....

System O/P State: ....

Test Procedure

1. ....

2. ....

3. ....

4. ....

Test Verification

....

....

....

Test Result: Accepted   Not Accepted

Test Executed By   ....

Date/Time   ....

Comments   ....

....

....

FIGURE 11.1. Typical Test Case Form.

for functionality but also for its aesthetics (also known as ergonomics of a system).

The following attributes must be considered during human factors testing[Hob95][Nie96]. These factor are applicable to web-based applications as well.

Correctness: The actions associated with buttons and menus are correct. There is no ambiguity about the function of a button or a menu item.

Completeness: The interface provides all the necessary controls and functionality desired by the users. No functionality is missing from the interface.

Consistency: The application provides a consistent behavior throughout. If the software is being developed for internal use, the application interface must be consistent with other applications in the company. If the application is being developed for a commercial vendor, the interface should be consistent with the interface of the vendor's other products.

Easy Navigation: The user must be able to reach the desired area of application easily, not get lost in a stack of application screens. Also, the user must be able to get back to the first screen from anywhere in the application.

Conformance to Business Flow: Application flow conforms to the desired business flow.

Efficiency: The response to a user action is swift, direct, and efficient.

Interactive: The user is constantly updated on what the application is doing; user is never given the feeling that the application is not doing anything, or is stuck.

Aesthetics: The application uses pleasing colors and graphics. Shocking colors should be avoided.

Mouse/Keyboard Equivalence: Any action that can be performed with a mouse can also be performed with a keystroke.

Resolution Independence: The look and feel of the application are independent of the screen resolution.

Platform Independence: The look and feel of the application are independent of the platform. The clients on PCs and UNIX should not see a difference in the interface.

On-Line Help: The application consistently provides context-sensitive on-line help.

Exception Handling: Exceptions are handled gracefully, and visual, and possibly audio, feedback is provided to the user.

Reserved Words: The application does not use reserved words for non-standard actions. Examples of reserved words include *Cancel,* and *Quit.*

11.3.4   Performance Testing

A system may perform all its functions in a satisfactory manner and yet fail to meet the user's expectations[Hun96a]. This can easily happen if the performance requirements of a system were overlooked during its design and implementation. Let us consider a noncritical database querying system. If the user has to wait for minutes[6] for an answer, the system is most likely going to be trashed even though it produces the correct results. Similarly, a slow or poor response in medical and flight control system can jeopardize

---

[6]It has been observed that an average user on the internet does not wait more than 15 seconds for a page to load in the browser.

human lives and is completely unacceptable. Hence, it is imperative that the performance requirements be completely and clearly specified during requirements collection and analysis. At the system testing stage all of these performance requirements must be completely regression tested.[7]

An important factor during performance testing is a controlled test environment. System performance must be measured under varying external factors like network traffic, server load, client machine activity, database activity, and time of day. A typical set of activities for system performance testing follows.

Select a Use Case: Select a use case that requires its functionality to be executed within a given time interval. For many use cases such a time constraint may not have been specified. In such cases, testers, in consultation with the system users, should come up with a performance requirement.Every use case should be performance tested and the resulting statistics logged.

Select Input Values and Initial States: Select a subset of input values and a subset of system initial states. to be used for performance testing. Note that these input values are a subset of the input values used during functional testing. Similarly, the initial states are a subset of the initial states used during functional testing.

Select Single Input and Initial State: Select a single input value and an initial system state. These are the constants for the next few test cases. Execute the primary use case under these conditions. Monitor the performance of the system under the given external variables, which may include the following.

- test machine memory utilization
- test machine swap space utilization
- test machine CPU utilization
- network traffic
- other applications running on the test machine
- server machine load
- client machine load
- database load
- time of day

Vary Input Values: Repeat the previous step by keeping the same initial state and external variables while varying the input values.

Vary Initial States: Repeat the same step with the same input values and external variables while varying the initial states of the system.

Vary External Factors: Retest system performance by varying the external factors. This will give the testers a feeling of when the system

---

[7]We assume that the system is performance tested during its development.

performance starts to degrade and whether it is acceptable under the given requirements.

11.3.5   Capacity Testing

One type of performance capability testing of a system is known as *volume* testing[Het88]. Although there are subtle differences in their definitions, we use the terms *volume,* testing and *load* testing synonymously.

The purpose of volume and stress testing is to determine the extreme capabilities of a system. Volume and stress testing are two types of capacity testing. Volume testing is planned with the specific objective of determining how many transactions and/or how many users can be operationally supported by a system. Functional test cases that have already been successfully tested are executed with higher and higher volumes until the system is no longer capable of effective operation.

The objective of Stress Testing is to show that the system has the capacity to process large numbers of transactions during peak periods. "Peak period" may mean the maximum utilization time of the day for a system. This testing would be purposely designed to pit various kinds against each other in competition for system resources. The performance and scalability of an application should be measured under dire conditions[Str96].

The approach used for volume and stress testing is to check the system at a higher level of abstraction. Consider the transaction processing system on page 129. While processing a transaction file, the result of the transaction processing does not determine the outcome of the test case. Instead, the total number of transactions handled is perused to arbitrate the result of the test case. The system under test is driven to its capacity to ascertain the threshold at which the system breaks down. A system is driven to its limit in terms of the following attributes[Bas96].

Concurrent Passive Users: A *passive* user may be defined as a user that has started up the system but is not utilizing the functional capabilities of the system. The system under test must be loaded with volumes of concurrent passive users to determine its threshold.

Concurrent Active Users: An *active* user is the one that utilizes the functional capabilities of a system at a given time. The capacity of the system to handle maximum concurrent active users must also be established.

Concurrent Application Activities for a Single User: A system may define an upper limit on the number of concurrent functional capabilities of a system, for example, how many users can concurrently create a new order in the system.

Concurrent Database Access: If a system is heavily database oriented, an information system for example, the number of concurrent databases that can be accessed may be limited.

Maximum Data Volume: The maximum expected data volume within a given time interval must be considered.

Storage Requirements: Required storage for large volumes of data should be checked.

Varying Functionality Concurrency: Concurrent execution of possibly conflicting and competing functional capabilities of a system must be performed. Two functional capabilities of a system may compete for system resources.

Same Functionality Concurrency: Concurrent execution of the same functionality of a system must be tested.

External Factors: System functionality should be executed while varying the system environment to its extreme. A system can be tested, for example, while keeping the CPU utilization at 100 percent.

Volume and stress testing require massive amounts of test data. Tools like data generators can be very useful during these types of testing activities.

11.3.6 Documentation Testing

One of the most critical pieces of a software system is the documentation. Traditionally, the documentation that accompanies a delivered system is very poor. Manuals are created either too late or too early, and hence do not correctly reflect the current state of the software system. If object-oriented systems are to improve the quality of delivered systems, the development team must greatly improve the quality of the documentation as well. Documentation testing requires that the documentation be checked for its correctness, consistency, clarity, and validity. Documentation associated with a system include system design and development documents, user manuals, training material, system start-up/stop procedures, system error catalogs, on-line help, system operations, developer's guides, and system maintenance documents.

Documents should be tested throughout the different types of system testing activities. During sanity testing, for example, system start-up/stop procedures given in the operations manuals should be followed to the letter to determine their accuracy. Any discrepancies should be noted and reported.

It must be remembered that the objective of documentation testing is to validate the conformance of documentation with the observable behavior of the system under test. Some of the significant issues to be considered during documentation testing follow.

Accuracy A procedure outlined in the document accurately depicts the system behavior.

Steps Completeness All of the steps are outlined in a given procedure. Steps should not be missing. Similarly, no assumptions are made about the minor steps in a procedure.

Clarity Each step in a procedure is clearly specified without any assumptions or shortcuts.

Conformance All screen captures accurately represent the displayed screens.

Procedures Completeness No procedures are missing from documentation.

Referential Integrity References to other document numbers and names are accurate.

Correct Indices Proper indices and table of contents are included in the documentation.

Reference Document A central reference document for ease of finding the required procedures and operations is supplied.

Exceptional Handling Response of the system in case of failures is correctly specified.

Vocabulary All terms are clearly defined and abbreviations are given before the terms.

11.4   Resources

System testing consumes significant resources, and that's the way it should be. The complexity of the system testing phase is such that significant personnel and computer resources must be utilized to do an effective job. The resources should not be used ineffectively, however; two persons should not be assigned a job that can be done by only one person. The management of system testing is a challenging undertaking and must be planned and executed very carefully.

Although resources for system testing are highly system dependent, we present a general set of resources that would probably be used for most system testing activities.

Test Environment A test environment closely resembling the final production environment is of the foremost importance to avoid surprises in production system. Creating a test environment that is an exact replica of the production environment may be asking a little too much; in the real world, there are always differences between a production environment and the test environment. However, one should try to create as close a replica as possible. For some systems it is not possible to create a production like environment, an air traffic control system, for example. For such systems simulator tools must be employed. Similarly, for a system that will have a large userbase, a heavy load of users has to be simulated for stress and volume testing.

Tools With the increased complexity of today's software systems, a battery of automated tools is almost a necessity for effective system testing.

The sheer volume of test cases and test data for a nontrivial system makes manual testing an impossible task.[8] Even with the help of tools, a system cannot be tested for all possible conditions. Tools exponentially increase the possible conditions that a system can be tested under. Following are some of the helpful tools during the system testing stage[Het88]. For a detailed list of general software testing tools see Perry[Per95]. Note that some of these tools are on our wish list and are not commercially available.

- **Instrumentors** aid in measuring and reporting test coverage. Some possible coverage criteria for object-oriented systems are use case coverage, class coverage, interface coverage intraclass methods interaction coverage, and requirements coverage.
- **Comparators** help in comparing various outputs of a system. For an object-oriented system, comparators should include object state comparators and system state comparators etc.
- **Data Generators** are used for generating volumes of data for various forms of capacity testing.
- **Record-Playback Tools** are utilized for testing user interfaces (UIs). This is one of the most commonly available commercial tools.
- **Simulators** come in handy for simulating environments that would otherwise be impossible to create. Consider, for example, a system with a few thousand concurrent users or an air traffic control system.
- **Software Problems Tracking Tools** for tracking the life cycle of a reported error.
- **Environment Monitors** help in monitoring the environment variables. These tools may include memory and CPU utilization monitors, network traffic monitors, database transactions monitors, system load monitors, and so on.

Test Team: A test team is made up of members of the project team. Each member of the test team brings his/her perspective as well as his/her expertise that to the task of towards increasing the quality of the desired product. Some of the possible roles in a test team are:

- software integrator(s)
- software coordinator(s)
- domain expert(s)
- product or quality assurance personnel
- network administrator(s)
- system administrator(s)
- system architect(s)
- system developer(s)

---

[8]Although the Quality Assurance Institute believes that as much as 80 percent of all software is tested manually[Bak94].

Depending on the nature and size of the project, each of these roles may be played by a single or many persons. Some of the roles may be played by a single person. For example, system coordinator and system integrator could possibly be one person.

Test Coordinator: One person on the testing team must assume the role of test coordinator. One of the major responsibilities of the coordinator is to ensure coordination among the different members of the test team in the necessary preparation, test execution, and the following up of the reported errors.

11.5 Effort

According to Perry[Per95], system testing is only up to 80 percent effective in detecting software bugs. Effective use of the parallel testing model described in figure 2.3, prevents many defects from entering the system testing phase. This in turn helps in reducing the number of software defects entering the production or maintenance phase.

Regardless of any necessary measures and precautions, there are always bugs in the software entering the system testing phase. As a general rule, one third of the development effort should be expended during the system testing phase. Hence, if it takes a year to get the product ready for system testing, approximately four months should be spent in testing the system. Obviously, this time period is a ball park figure and can be altered depending on a project needs and the target domain for the software. Some software for example life-saving equipment software, would need more thorough testing than others.

11.6 Acceptance Criteria

The most obvious criterion for judging the completion of the system testing phase is the system readiness for the intended production environment. The readiness of a system depends on the priorities of the system. Some of the priorities include functionality, reliability, availability, and performance.

Critical business applications require reliable software. Reliability can be defined as the probability of a system operating without failure over a specified time under certain operating conditions. Developing reliable software is one of the biggest challenges facing the software industry today[Woo96]. If reliability is the biggest priority for the system, then an appropriate reliability growth model can provide useful information about the readiness of a system for production.

Establishing a software system's readiness for production is an arduous task. There are two basic approaches to it, *informal*, and *formal*. The *informal* approach involves getting the approval of a representative set of intended customers in the testing process. Once these customers have agreed that they are ready to accept the software in a production environment, software is shipped. This approach obviously is well suited for a small, known customer base. Software systems developed for an organization's internal use may use this approach.

For most commercial software systems, however, a rigorous, *formal*, and mathematical approach is more suitable. *Software reliability growth models* help in performing the task. The models are mathematical functions that describe defect detection rates. These models can be classified into two broad categories, *concave* and *S-shaped*[Woo96]. *Concave* models include the Goel-Okumoto[GO79], Hossain-Dahiya[HD93], Pareto[Lit81], Weibull[MIO87], and Yamada Exponential[YOO86] models. *S-shaped* models include the G-O S-Shaped [YOO83], Gompertz[Kec91], and Yamada Raleigh[YOO86] models.

The difference between the two types of models is that S-shaped models assume that early testing is not as efficient as later testing. The asymptotic behavior of both types of models is very similar, however. The defect detection rate in both types of models decreases as the number of detected defects increases. Depending on the type of software being developed, a suitable defect detection rate can be chosen as the point where software can be shipped to the target customers.

11.7 Summary

System testing is not limited to testing the functionality embedded in software code. System testing tests the whole system. A system must be sanity tested to ensure proper start-up and shut-down. A system must be thoroughly tested for functional completeness, functional correctness, and functional consistency. A system's performance must be examined against its performance requirements. A system must be load tested for heavy volumes of data and users to determine its scalability. A system must be tested for its liveness by operating it for hours, days, or months to identify deadlocks and/or nontermination. A system must be checked for its portability across a range of hardware/software platforms thatit may execute. The human factors aspect of a system must be examined to determine its usability and user friendliness. A system's documentation must be comprehensively checked for its correctness, consistency with the system, and completeness.

All these aspects of a software system contribute toward user satisfaction with a system. If users are unhappy with one aspect of a system, ten other good features of the system will be ignored. Comprehensive system testing can ensure that the software system delivered to its intended users conforms with its explicit and implicit requirements. Even though, the system components are tested throughout the software development process, the intricacies of the final system testing phase should never be underestimated. This stage provides the final opportunity for a development team to tune the system before it goes live. Ample resources and time must be allocated to this phase.

Appendix A
SampleStatistic Class Source Code

The source code for the `SampleStatistic` class as taken from `libg++`[Lea92] is provided here for reference.

A.1   Header File

```
// This may look like C code, but it is really -*- C++ -*-
/*
Copyright (C) 1988 Free Software Foundation
    written by Dirk Grunwald (grunwald@cs.uiuc.edu)

This file is part of the GNU C++ Library.  This library is free
software; you can redistribute it and/or modify it under the terms of
the GNU Library General Public License as published by the Free
Software Foundation; either version 2 of the License, or (at your
option) any later version.  This library is distributed in the hope
that it will be useful, but WITHOUT ANY WARRANTY; without even the
implied warranty of MERCHANTABILITY or FITNESS FOR A PARTICULAR
PURPOSE.  See the GNU Library General Public License for more details.
You should have received a copy of the GNU Library General Public
License along with this library; if not, write to the Free Software
Foundation, 59 Temple Place - Suite 330, Boston, MA 02111-
1307, USA.
*/
```

```
#ifndef SampleStatistic_h
#ifdef __GNUG__
#pragma interface
#endif
#define SampleStatistic_h 1

#include <builtin.h>

#undef min
#undef max

class SampleStatistic {
protected:
    int n;
    double x;
    double x2;
    double minValue, maxValue;

    public :

    SampleStatistic();
    inline virtual ~SampleStatistic();
    virtual void reset();

    virtual void operator+=(double);
    int samples();
    double mean();
    double stdDev();
    double var();
    double min();
    double max();
    double confidence(int p_percentage);
    double confidence(double p_value);

    void error(const char* msg);
};

// error handlers

extern void default_SampleStatistic_error_handler(const char*);
extern one_arg_error_handler_t SampleStatistic_error_handler;

extern one_arg_error_handler_t
        set_SampleStatistic_error_handler(one_arg_error_handler_t f);
```

```
inline SampleStatistic:: SampleStatistic(){ reset();}
inline int SampleStatistic:: samples() {return(n);}
inline double SampleStatistic:: min() {return(minValue);}
inline double SampleStatistic:: max() {return(maxValue);}
inline SampleStatistic::~SampleStatistic() {}

#endif
```

A.2   Source File

```
// This may look like C code, but it is really -*- C++ -*-
/*
Copyright (C) 1988 Free Software Foundation
    written by Dirk Grunwald (grunwald@cs.uiuc.edu)

This file is part of the GNU C++ Library.  This library is free
software; you can redistribute it and/or modify it under the terms of
the GNU Library General Public License as published by the Free
Software Foundation; either version 2 of the License, or (at your
option) any later version.  This library is distributed in the hope
that it will be useful, but WITHOUT ANY WARRANTY; without even the
implied warranty of MERCHANTABILITY or FITNESS FOR A PARTICULAR
PURPOSE.  See the GNU Library General Public License for more details.
You should have received a copy of the GNU Library General Public
License along with this library; if not, write to the Free Software
Foundation, 59 Temple Place - Suite 330, Boston, MA 02111-
1307, USA.
*/
#ifdef __GNUG__
#pragma implementation
#endif
#include <stream.h>
#include <SmplStat.h>
#include <math.h>

#ifndef HUGE_VAL
#ifdef HUGE
#define HUGE_VAL HUGE
#else
#include <float.h>
#define HUGE_VAL DBL_MAX
#endif
#endif
```

// error handling

```
void default_SampleStatistic_error_handler(const char* msg)
{
  cerr << "Fatal SampleStatistic error. " << msg << "\n";
  exit(1);
}

one_arg_error_handler_t SampleStatistic_error_handler =
default_SampleStatistic_error_handler;

one_arg_error_handler_t
set_SampleStatistic_error_handler(one_arg_error_handler_t f)
{
  one_arg_error_handler_t old = SampleStatistic_error_handler;
  SampleStatistic_error_handler = f;
  return old;
}

void SampleStatistic::error(const char* msg)
{
  (*SampleStatistic_error_handler)(msg);
}
```

// t-distribution: given p-value and degrees of freedom, return t-value
// adapted from Peizer & Pratt JASA, vol63, p1416

```
double tval(double p, int df)
{
  double t;
  int positive = p >= 0.5;
  p = (positive)? 1.0 - p : p;
  if (p <= 0.0 || df <= 0)
    t = HUGE_VAL;
  else if (p == 0.5)
    t = 0.0;
  else if (df == 1)
    t = 1.0 / tan((p + p) * 1.57079633);
  else if (df == 2)
    t = sqrt(1.0 / ((p + p) * (1.0 - p)) - 2.0);
  else
  {
    double ddf = df;
    double a = sqrt(log(1.0 / (p * p)));
```

```
    double aa = a * a;
    a = a - ((2.515517 + (0.802853 * a) + (0.010328 * aa)) /
            (1.0 + (1.432788 * a) + (0.189269 * aa) +
            (0.001308 * aa * a)));
    t = ddf - 0.666666667 + 1.0 / (10.0 * ddf);
    t = sqrt(ddf * (exp(a * a * (ddf - 0.833333333) / (t * t)) - 1.0));
    }
    return (positive)? t : -t;
}

void
SampleStatistic::reset()
{
    n = 0; x = x2 = 0.0;
    maxValue = -HUGE_VAL;
    minValue = HUGE_VAL;
}

void
SampleStatistic::operator+=(double value)
{
    n += 1;
    x += value;
    x2 += (value * value);
    if ( minValue > value) minValue = value;
    if ( maxValue < value) maxValue = value;
}

double
SampleStatistic::mean()
{
    if ( n > 0) {
        return (x / n);
    }
    else {
        return ( 0.0 );
    }
}

double
SampleStatistic::var()
{
    if ( n > 1) {
        return(( x2 - ((x * x) / n)) / ( n - 1));
    }
```

```
    else {
        return ( 0.0 );
    }
}

double
SampleStatistic::stdDev()
{
    if ( n ≤ 0 || this → var() ≤ 0) {
        return(0);
    } else {
        return( (double) sqrt( var() ) );
    }
}

double
SampleStatistic::confidence(int interval)
{
  int df = n - 1;
  if (df ≤ 0) return HUGE_VAL;
  double t = tval(double(100 + interval) * 0.005, df);
  if (t == HUGE_VAL)
    return t;
  else
    return (t * stdDev()) / sqrt(double(n));
}

double
SampleStatistic::confidence(double p_value)
{
  int df = n - 1;
  if (df ≤ 0) return HUGE_VAL;
  double t = tval((1.0 + p_value) * 0.5, df);
  if (t == HUGE_VAL)
    return t;
  else
    return (t * stdDev()) / sqrt(double(n));
}
```

Appendix B
SampleHistogram Class Source Code

The source code for the `SampleHistogram` class as taken from `libg++`[Lea92] is provided here for reference.

B.1 Header File

// This may look like C code, but it is really -*- C++ -*-
/*
Copyright (C) 1988 Free Software Foundation
*   written by Dirk Grunwald (grunwald@cs.uiuc.edu)*

This file is part of the GNU C++ Library.   This library is free
software; you can redistribute it and/or modify it under the terms of
the GNU Library General Public License as published by the Free
Software Foundation; either version 2 of the License, or (at your
option) any later version.   This library is distributed in the hope
that it will be useful, but WITHOUT ANY WARRANTY; without even the
implied warranty of MERCHANTABILITY or FITNESS FOR A PARTICULAR
PURPOSE.   See the GNU Library General Public License for more details.
You should have received a copy of the GNU Library General Public
License along with this library; if not, write to the Free Software
Foundation, 59 Temple Place - Suite 330, Boston, MA 02111-
1307, USA.
*/

```
#ifndef SampleHistogram_h
#ifdef __GNUG__
#pragma interface
#endif
#define SampleHistogram_h 1

#include <iostream.h>
#include <SmplStat.h>
```

extern const int SampleHistogramMinimum;
extern const int SampleHistogramMaximum;

class SampleHistogram : **public** SampleStatistic
{
protected:
    short howManyBuckets;
    int *bucketCount;
    double *bucketLimit;

public:

    SampleHistogram(**double** low, **double** hi, **double** bucketWidth =
-1.0);

    ~SampleHistogram();

    virtual void reset();
    virtual void operator+=(double);

    int similarSamples(**double**);

    int buckets();

    double bucketThreshold(**int** i);
    int inBucket(**int** i);
    void printBuckets(ostream&);

};

inline int SampleHistogram:: buckets() { **return**(howManyBuckets); };

inline double SampleHistogram:: bucketThreshold(**int** i) {
    if (i < 0 || i ≥ howManyBuckets)

```
            error("invalid bucket access");
        return(bucketLimit[i]);
}

inline int SampleHistogram:: inBucket(int i) {
    if (i < 0 || i ≥ howManyBuckets)
        error("invalid bucket access");
    return(bucketCount[i]);
}

#endif
```

B.2   Source File

```
// This may look like C code, but it is really -*- C++ -*-
/*
Copyright (C) 1988 Free Software Foundation
    written by Dirk Grunwald (grunwald@cs.uiuc.edu)

This file is part of the GNU C++ Library.  This library is free
software; you can redistribute it and/or modify it under the terms of
the GNU Library General Public License as published by the Free
Software Foundation; either version 2 of the License, or (at your
option) any later version.  This library is distributed in the hope
that it will be useful, but WITHOUT ANY WARRANTY; without even the
implied warranty of MERCHANTABILITY or FITNESS FOR A PARTICULAR
PURPOSE.  See the GNU Library General Public License for more details.
You should have received a copy of the GNU Library General Public
License along with this library; if not, write to the Free Software
Foundation, 59 Temple Place - Suite 330, Boston, MA 02111-
1307, USA.
*/
#ifdef __GNUG__
#pragma implementation
#endif
#include <stream.h>
#include <SmplHist.h>
#include <math.h>

#ifndef HUGE_VAL
#ifdef HUGE
#define HUGE_VAL HUGE
#else
```

```
#include <float.h>
#define HUGE_VAL DBL_MAX
#endif
#endif

const int SampleHistogramMinimum = -2;
const int SampleHistogramMaximum = -1;

SampleHistogram::SampleHistogram(double low, double high, double
width)
{
    if (high < low) {
        double t = high;
        high = low;
        low = t;
    }

    if (width == -1) {
        width = (high - low) / 10;
    }

    howManyBuckets = int((high - low) / width) + 2;
    bucketCount = new int[howManyBuckets];
    bucketLimit = new double[howManyBuckets];
    double lim = low;
    for (int i = 0; i < howManyBuckets; i++) {
        bucketCount[i] = 0;
        bucketLimit[i] = lim;
        lim += width;
    }
    bucketLimit[howManyBuckets-1] = HUGE_VAL; /* from math.h */
}

SampleHistogram::~SampleHistogram()
{
    if (howManyBuckets > 0) {
        delete bucketCount;
        delete bucketLimit;
    }
}

void
SampleHistogram::operator+=(double value)
{
    int i;
```

```
    for (i = 0; i < howManyBuckets; i++) {
        if (value < bucketLimit[i]) break;
    }
    bucketCount[i]++;
    this→SampleStatistic::operator+=(value);
}

int
SampleHistogram::similarSamples(double d)
{
    int i;
    for (i = 0; i < howManyBuckets; i++) {
        if (d < bucketLimit[i]) return(bucketCount[i]);
    }
    return(0);
}

void
SampleHistogram::printBuckets(ostream& s)
{
    for(int i = 0; i < howManyBuckets; i++) {
        if (bucketLimit[i] >= HUGE_VAL) {
            s << "< max : " << bucketCount[i] << "\n";
        } else {
            s << "< " << bucketLimit[i] << " : " << bucketCount[i] <<
"\n";
        }
    }
}

void
SampleHistogram::reset()
{
    this→SampleStatistic::reset();
    if (howManyBuckets > 0) {
        for (register int i = 0; i < howManyBuckets; i++) {
            bucketCount[i] = 0;
        }
    }
}
```

Appendix C
PriorityQueue Class Source Code

The `PriorityQueue` class implementation, in both Eiffel and C++ is provided here.

C.1 Eiffel Implementation

```
Class PQ export
   length{PQ}, add, delete, largest{PQ}, eqn
inherit
   STD_FILES
feature
   MAX_LEN: INTEGER is 250;
   array: ARRAY[INTEGER];
   length: INTEGER;

   Create is
     do
        array.Create(1,MAX_LEN)
     end; -- Create

   largest: INTEGER is
     require
       length > 0
     do
```

```
      Result := array.entry(1)
   end; -- largest

add(x: INTEGER) is
   local
      parent_ptr, child_ptr,
      parent, child: INTEGER;
      stop: BOOLEAN
   do
      length := length + 1;
      array.enter(length, x);
      from
         child_ptr := length;
      until
         child_ptr < 2 or stop
      loop
         parent_ptr := child_ptr div 2;
         child := array.entry(child_ptr);
         parent := array.entry(parent_ptr);
         if parent ≥ child then
            stop := true
         else
            array.enter(parent_ptr, child);
            array.enter(child_ptr, parent);
            child_ptr := parent_ptr;
         end; -- if
      end; -- loop
   end; -- a

   -- Buggy delete
delete is
   local
      parent_ptr, child_ptr,
      l_child_ptr, r_child_ptr: INTEGER;
      parent, child: INTEGER;
      stop: BOOLEAN
   do
      if length > 0 then
         -- Move the last element to the first
         array.enter(1, array.entry(length));
         length := length - 1;

         from
            parent_ptr := 1;
            l_child_ptr := 2 * parent_ptr;
```

```
            r_child_ptr := 2 * parent_ptr + 1
        until
            stop or l_child_ptr ≥ length
        -————————∧-———-
        -- The correct statement is --
        -- stop or l_child_ptr > length --
        -————————————

        loop
            -- find proper child
            if ((l_child_ptr = length) or else
                (array.entry(l_child_ptr) >
                (array.entry(r_child_ptr))))) then
                child_ptr := l_child_ptr
            else
                child_ptr := r_child_ptr
            end; -- if

            parent := array.entry(parent_ptr);
            child := array.entry(child_ptr);
            if parent < (child) then
                -- swap
                array.enter(parent_ptr, child);
                array.enter(child_ptr, parent);
                parent_ptr := child_ptr;
                l_child_ptr := parent_ptr * 2;
                r_child_ptr := l_child_ptr + 1
            else
                stop := true
            end; -- if
        end; -- loop
    end; -- if
end; -- d


eqn (other: like Current): BOOLEAN is
    local
        stop: BOOLEAN
    do
        if other.Void then
            Result := false
        else
            if length = other.length then
                from
                until
                    length = 0 or stop
                loop
```

```
            if largest = other.largest then
                delete; other.delete
            else
                stop := true
            end; -- if
        end; -- loop
        Result := not stop
    else
        Result := false
    end; -- if
  end; -- if
end; -- eqn


end; -- Class PQ
```

C.2   C++ Header File

```
// -*- C++ -*-
/*——————*/
/*— PQ.h —*/
/*——————*/
/*
 * Responsibility:
 * Role:
 * Communications:
 * Bugs & Caveats:
 * Maintainer:
 *
 * $Id$
 * $Log$
 *
 *
 */


#ifndef _PQ_h
#define _PQ_h 1

#include <std.h>
#include <stream.h>

#define MAX_LENGTH 10
```

```
enum bool{false, true};

class PQ {
  public:
    PQ();
    ~PQ();
    void add(int num);
    void remove();
    bool empty();
    int largest();
    int length(){ return _length;}
    void print();

  private:
    int *pq;
    int _length;

};

#endif
```

C.3   C++ Source File

```
// -*- C++ -*-
/*————*/
/*— PQ.cc —*/
/*————*/
/*
 * Synopsis:
 * Implementation Notes:
 * ToDo:
 *
 * $Id$
 * $Log$
 *
 *
 */

#include "PQ.h"

PQ::PQ()
{
```

```
    _length = 0;
    pq = new int[MAX_LENGTH];
}

PQ::~PQ()
{
}


void PQ::add(int num)
{
    int childIndex, parentIndex, child, parent;
    bool stop;

    // because of indexing of trees, we dont store anything
    // at the zero-th index of the pq array

    if(_length < MAX_LENGTH) {
        pq[++_length] = num;

        childIndex=_length;
        stop = false;

        while((childIndex >= 2) && (stop==false)){
            parentIndex = childIndex/2;
            child = pq[childIndex];
            parent = pq[parentIndex];
            if(parent >= child){
                stop = true;
            }
            else {
                pq[parentIndex] = child;
                pq[childIndex] = parent;
                childIndex = parentIndex;
            }
        }
    }
}


void PQ::remove()
{
    int childIndex, parentIndex, child, parent;
    int lChildIndex, rChildIndex;
    bool stop;
```

```
if(_length>0) {

    // move the last element to the first
    pq[1] = pq[_length--];

    parentIndex = 1;
    lChildIndex = 2 * parentIndex;
    rChildIndex = 2 * parentIndex + 1;
    stop = false;

    while((lChildIndex < _length) && (stop == false)) {

        // find proper child
        if((lChildIndex == _length) || (pq[lChildIndex] >
pq[rChildIndex]))
            childIndex = lChildIndex;
        else
            childIndex = rChildIndex;

        parent = pq[parentIndex];
        child = pq[childIndex];

        if(parent < child) {
            // swap
            pq[parentIndex] = child;
            pq[childIndex] = parent;
            parentIndex = childIndex;
            lChildIndex = parentIndex * 2;
            rChildIndex = lChildIndex + 1;
        }
        else
            stop = true;
    }
  }
}


int PQ::largest()
{
    if(_length>0)
        return pq[1];
}
```

```cpp
bool PQ::empty()
{
    if(_length==0)
        return true;
    else
        return false;
}

void PQ::print()
{
    for(int i=1; i<=_length; i++)
        cout << pq[i] << "\n";
    cout << "------------------" << "\n";
}
```

Appendix D
Algorithms for Drawing MaDUM

Pseudo algorithm for drawing the MaDUM of a class is given here.

D.1 Base Class MaDUM Algorithm

Following is a procedure for drawing the minimal data members usage matrix of a class under test.

Let K = class under test. Then

$$ECG(K) = \langle M(K), D(K), E_{md}, E_{mm} \rangle,$$

where $M(K), D(K)$ and E_{md}, E_{mm} are as defined on pages 51 and 56, respectively.

Let U be the set of methods of a class such that each method directly uses at least one data member of the class. Mathematically,

$$U = \{m_i | (m_i, d_j) \in E_{md}\}$$

Let $\sharp$ represent the *cardinality*[1] of a set. Then

$$n_m = \sharp(M(K))$$

$$n_d = \sharp(D(K))$$

$$n_u = \sharp(U)$$

---

[1] The technical term *cardinality* denotes the number of elements in a finite set.

$MaDUM = DUM[n_d][n_m]$
$DUM_i = i$-th level usage of data members by member functions

// 1. Create first-level usage DUM.
```
  i = 0;

  for(x=0; x< nu; x++) {
    for(y=0; y< nd; y++) {
```

$$DUM_i[d_y][m_x] = \begin{cases} t_0 & \text{if method } m_x \rightsquigarrow \text{data member } d_y \\\\ r_0 & \text{if } m_x \text{ reports the state of } d_y \\\\ o_0 & \text{if } m_x \,@@\, d_y \\\\ & \text{else} \end{cases}$$

```
    }
  }
```

// 2. While U is not empty, create the next-level usage of
// DUM by readjusting U such that each member of U_new
// is a parent of some member of U_old.

```
  while(U != ∅) {

    i++;

    Utemp = ∅;

    for(x=0; x< nu; x++) {
      // A ℘ B ⟹ A is parent-of B.
      if(mj ℘ mx)
        Utemp = Utemp ∪ mj;
    }

    U = Utemp;

    for(x=0; x< nu; x++) {
      Cmx = {mk | mx ℘ mk};
      for(y=0; y< nd; y++) {
        DUMi[dy][mx] = ⋃j=0^♯(Cmx) DUMi-1[dy][mj];
      }
```

```
        }
    }
```

```
// 3. Combine all DUM's
    DUM = ⋃ᵢⱼ₌₀ DUMⱼ;
```

```
// 4. Minimize MaDUM: If there is no change in the number
// of usages of a data member, when going from a child-node
// to parent-node, then the entry of the parent node is
// redundant and hence can be removed.
    for(x=0; x< n_d; x++) {
        B_x = branch from d_x to root-node ;
        L_x = number of levels in B_x ;
        for(y=2; y< L_x; y++) {
            // Two entries are approximately equal(≈) if they differ
            // only in the values of their subscripts.
            if(DUM[d_x][m_{y-1}] ≈ DUM[d_x][m_y])
                DUM[d_x][m_y] = Redundant;
        }
    }
```

```
// 5. Remove redundant entries.
    for(x=0; x< n_d; x++) {
        for(y=0; y< n_m; y++) {
            if(DUM[d_x][m_y] == redundant)
                removeEntry(DUM[d_x][m_y]);
        }
    }
```

```
// 6. You have a minimal data members usage matrix.
    MaDUM = DUM;
```

D.2   Derived Class MaDUM Algorithm

Following is a procedure for drawing the minimal data members usage matrix of a derived class under test.

Let

S = sub-class under test

K = base-class of class S

$ECG(S) = \langle M(S), D(S), E_{md}, E_{mm}, U_d(K), U_m(K) \rangle$

$M(S), D(S), E_{md}, E_{mm}$ are the same as given in figure D.

$U_d(K) = \{d_{ik} \mid (m_{js}, d_{ik}) \in E_{md}\}$

$U_m(K) = \{m_{ik} \mid (m_{js}, m_{ik}) \; in E_{mm}\}$

$n_{mk} = \sharp(M(K))$

$n_{dk} = \sharp(D(K))$

$n_{ms} = \sharp(M(S)$

$n_{ds} = \sharp(D(S))$

$MaDUM_k = DUM[n_{dk}][n_{mk}]$

// 1. Extend the MaDUM of base class to create the MaDUM of the derived class.

$$MaDUM_s = DUM[n_{dk} + n_{ds}][n_{mk} + n_{ms}]$$

// 2. Fill the MaDUM one quadrant at a time.
// 2.1 Fill Quadrant II by using combined DUM of the base class.

// 2.2 Fill Quadrant IV by using the algorithm
// in section D.1.

$$DUM_{IV} = DUM[n_{ds}][n_{ms}]$$

// 2.3 Fill Quadrant III.

$$MaDUM_{III} = DUM[n_{ds}][n_{mk}]$$

// 2.3.1 Determine the methods that have been
// redefined in the derived class.

$$M_{ks} = \{m_i \mid m_i \in M(K) \; And \; m_i \in M(S)\}$$

// 2.3.2 Determine the methods of base class
// that call these redefined methods.

$$M_{km} = \{m_j \mid m_i \in M_{ks} \; And \; m_j \; \wp \; m_i\}$$

// 2.3.3 Create the second level usage of the derived class data
// members by the member functions of the base class.

for(x=0; x< $n_{M_{km}}$; x++) {

$C_{m_x} = \{m_l \mid m_x \; \wp \; m_l \; And \; m_l \in M_{km}\}$;

// Take a union of columns of all derived class redefined methods

```
// and store it in the column of the calling method of the base class.
for(y=0; y< n_ds; y++) {
```

$$DUM[d_y][m_x] = \bigcup_{j=0}^{\#(C_{m_x})} DUM[d_y][m_j];$$

```
   }
}
```

// 2.3.4 Minimize MaDUM for Quadrant I similar to step 4 in section D.1

```
for(x=0; x< n_dk; x++) {
```

B_x = branch from d_{xk} to root-node ;

L_x = number of levels in B_x ;

```
   for(y=2; y< L_x; y++) {
      // Two entries are approximately equal (≈) if they
      // differ only in the values of their subscripts.
      if(DUM[d_x][m_{y-1}] ≈ DUM[d_x][m_y])
         DUM[d_x][m_y] = Redundant;
   }
}
```

// 2.3.5 Remove redundant entries.

```
for(x=0; x< n_dk; x++) {
   for(y=0; y< n_ms; y++) {
      if(DUM[d_x][m_y] == Redundant)
         removeEntry(DUM[d_x][m_y]);
   }
}
```

// 2.4 Fill Quadrant I:

$$DUM_I = DUM[n_{dk}][n_{ms}]$$

// 2.4.1 Mark the methods that use the data members of the base class directly.

```
for(x=0; x< n_{u_dk}; x++) {
   for(y=0; y< n_ms; y++) {
```

$$DUM_I[d_x][m_y] = \begin{cases} t_0 & \text{if method } m_y \rightsquigarrow \text{data member } d_x \\ r_0 & \text{if } m_y \text{ reports the state of } d_x \\ o_0 & \text{if } m_y \ @@ \ d_x \\ & \text{else} \end{cases}$$

```
   }
}
```

// 2.4.2 Similar to the algorithm in section D.1,
// create next-level usage DUM's for Quadrant I.

// *If a derived class method calls a base class method,*
// *then the column for the base class method is repeated*
// *in the column for the derived class method.*
// *Each data usage type subscript is also incremented by one.*

$U = U_m(K)$
$i = 0;$
while$(U != \emptyset)$ {
    i++;
    $U_{temp} = \emptyset;$

    for(x=0; x< n_u; x++) {
      // *A $\wp$ B $\Longrightarrow$ A is parent-of B.*
      // *Let U_{temp} be the set of those methods of the derived class*
      // *that call methods in set U.*
      if$(m_j \; \wp \; m_x)$
        $U_{temp} = U_{temp} \cup m_j;$
    }

    $U = U_{temp};$

    for(x=0; x< $n_{u_{temp}}$; x++) {
      $C_{m_x} = \{m_l \mid m_x \; \wp \; m_l\};$

      // *Take a union of columns of all children and store the*
      // *result in parent's column with appropriate subscripts.*
      for(y=0; y< n_{dk}; y++) {
        $DUM[d_y][m_x] = \bigcup_{j=0}^{\#(C_{m_x})} DUM[d_y][m_j];$
      }
    }
}

// *2.4.3 Mark redundant entries as for Quadrant IV in step 2.3.3.*

// *2.4.4 Remove redundant entries as for Quadrant IV in step 2.3.4.*

// *2.5 In Quadrant II, replace combined DUM by MaDUM of base class.*

// *3. MaDUM for derived class is ready.*

Appendix E
Test Data Adequacy Axioms

Weyuker[Wey86] developed a general axiomatic theory of test data adequacy. In her original paper, she proposed a set of eight axioms. Various adequacy criteria were then considered in the light of these axioms. Weyuker[Wey88] later extended this set of eight axioms to eleven. Perry and Kaiser[PK90] applied these axioms to object-oriented programming. They divided the original set of eleven axioms into two categories. The first category includes seven axioms that are "intuitively obvious," and the second category of four "not so obvious" axioms deal with the relationship between the parts of a program and the whole. They claimed that the common intuition about the reduction of effort in testing the programs using inherited code is invalid.

In this appendix, we list these test data adequacy axioms and their extensions to object-oriented programming. Then we discuss the extent to which they are satisfied by our unit testing approach.

E.1 "Obvious" Axioms

Following are the seven "obvious" axioms as reported by Perry and Kaiser[PK90]. These axioms apply equally to all programs regardless of the programming paradigm or the language used for implementation. These axioms are also independent of the testing approach used.

E.1.1   Applicability

For every program, there exists an adequate test set.

E.1.2   NonExhaustive Applicability

There is a program P and test set T such that P is adequately tested by T, and T is not an exhaustive test set.

E.1.3   Monotonicity

If T is adequate for P, and $T \subseteq T'$ then T' is adequate for P.

E.1.4   Inadequate Empty Set

The empty set is not an adequate test set for any program.

E.1.5   Renaming

Let P be a renaming of Q. Then T is adequate for P if and only if T is adequate for Q.

E.1.6   Complexity

For every n, there is a program P, such that P is adequately tested by a size n test set, but not by any size $n - 1$ test set.

E.1.7   Statement Coverage

If T is adequate for P, then T causes every *executable* statement of P to be executed.

E.2   "Not-so-obvious" Axioms

The four axioms in this category can be called *inadequacy* axioms since they expose inadequacy of a test data set. We shall use each of these axioms to scrutinize our unit testing strategy.

E.2.1   Antiextensionality

There are programs P and Q such that $P \equiv Q$, T is adequate for P, but T is not adequate for Q.

This axiom is obviously aimed at *structural* testing, not at *functional* testing. Thus, if two programs are functionally equivalent with different implementations, then clearly the coverage criteria for one may not be adequate for the other. Hence, the test data set for one may not be appropriate for the other.

Most of the object-oriented languages allow a derived class to replace an inherited method with its own method, with the same signature. This is known as *overriding* or *redefinition* of methods. Intuitively, one would expect the test data set required for the base class method to be adequate for the *redefined* method, since it has the same name and functionality. This is precisely what the antiextensionality axiom warns us about. Although, a derived class may have used the same interface as the one provided by a method in its base class, generally it will implement the interface differently. Therefore, the test data set that was adequate for the method of the base class cannot be reused as is.

The following example has been provided in Perry and Kaiser[PK90] and we shall see how our unit testing strategy handles it.

Figure E.1 shows a class C as a base class. Two versions of class D are also shown. Version 1 does not redefine a method M of the base class C, whereas the second version provides its own definition of method M and hence overrides the inherited method M.

Case I. Method Not Redefined: In the first version of class D, if the method M is invoked on an object of type D, then class C's M will be called. Let's see how our testing scheme handles this situation.

For the first version of class D, let A_m be a set of all data members of class C such that method $M()$ acts at these data members. Mathematically, let

$$A_m = \{d_i \mid m(C) \, @@ \, d_i\},$$

where $d_i \in D(C)$ and $m(C) = $ method M of class C. Then,

$$m(C) \text{ needs retesting} \iff \exists m(D) \mid m(D) \, @@ \, d_i \in A_m.$$

Thus method m of class C will need retesting if and only if it shares the data member usage with any member function of the derived class D. Let

$$M_{d_i}(D) = \{m_i \mid m_i \in M(D) \text{ and } m_i \, @@ \, d_i \in A_m\}.$$

Then

$$M_{d_i}(D) = \emptyset \implies \text{no restesting required for } m(C).$$

On the other hand, if $M_{d_i}(D)$ is not an emptyset($\emptyset$), let

$$M'_{d_i}(D) = T_{d_i}(C) \cup (M_{d_i}(D) - R_{d_i}(D)).$$

Then we create all permutations of $M'_{d_i}(D)$ and retest d_i for these possible transformations.

```
class C {
  public:
    M() { ...; }
    ...
};
```

// version 1 of class D

```
class D : public C {
  ...
};
```

// version 2 of class D

```
class D : public C {
  public:
    M() { ...; }
    ...
};
```

FIGURE E.1. Example for antiextensionality axiom.

Case II. Method Redefined: For the second version of class D, where method M has been redefined, our scheme supports the antiextensionality axiom. According to our unit testing strategy, the redefined method M requires two-way testing.

1. The redefined method M should be tested in class D's environment depending on the data member usage by M. It would be tested in relation to all those methods that share the usage of a data member of class D.
2. The newly defined method M should also be tested in the environment of its base class, which is class C in this case. Let B_{d_i} be a set of all data members of class C such that method $M()$ of class D acts at these data members. Mathematically, we can write

$$B_{d_i} = \{d_i \in D(C) \mid m(D) @@ d_i\}.$$

Then method m of class D will have to be tested with all the methods of class C that share data member usage with it. Thus, let

$$M_{d_i}(C) = \{m_i \in M(C) \mid m_i \text{ @@ } d_i\}.$$

Then

$$M_{d_i}(C) = \emptyset \Longrightarrow \text{No retesting required for } m(D) \text{ in class } C$$

On the other hand, if $M_{d_i}(C)$ is not an empty set($\emptyset$), then $m(D)$ will be retested will all the member functions of class C that share data members usage with $m(D)$.

E.2.2   General Multiple Change

There are programs P and Q which are the same shape, and a test set T such that T is adequate for P , but T is not adequate for Q.

Weyuker[Wey88] provides three transformation rules that can transform a program to another with the *same shape*. According to Weyuker,

Two programs are of the *same shape* if one can be transformed into the other by applying the following rules any number of times:

- Replace relational operator r1 in a predicate with relational operator r2.
- Replace constant c1 in a predicate or assignment statement with constant c2.
- Replace arithmetic operator a1 in an assignment statement with arithmetic operator a2.

All three rules are based on the structure of a program.

Perry and Kaiser[PK90] argue that this axiom can be mapped to a multiple-inheritance problem where the same component may be inherited along different ancestor paths. Their example is shown in figure E.2.

Perry and Kaiser consider two programs to be different but of the same shape if the order in which multiple base classes are listed is changed. C++, however, does not impose any precedence ordering of the base classes. Therefore the two versions of class D in figure E.2 are essentially the same. If both, class B and class C provide a method M with exactly the same signature, then a call to method M on an object of type D is ambiguous. The caller must explicitly specify either B's M or C's M. Therefore this example is not appropriate for C++ based applications.

Our strategy, however, takes care of a situation like this by considering each class separately. Method M of the base class would be retested in the environment of the derived class only if both classes share the usage of some common data members. This has been supported by Perry and Kaiser[PK90]. They claim that the inherited methods need not be retested in the derived class if the derived class "adds new instance variables and new methods and there are no interactions in either direction between the

```
class B {
  public:
    M() { ...; }
    ...
};

class C {
  public:
    M() { ...; }
    ...
};


// version 1 of class D


class D : public B, public C {
  ...
};


// version 2 of class D


class D : public C, public B {
  ...
};
```

FIGURE E.2. Example for general multiple change axiom

new instance variables and methods and any inherited instance variables and methods."

E.2.3   Antidecomposition

There exists a program P and component Q such that T is adequate for P, T' is the set of vectors of values that variables can assume on entrance to Q for some t in T, and T' is not adequate for Q.

This axiom, when extended to object-oriented programming, implies that when a new derived class is added (or an existing subclass is modified), the methods inherited from the base classes should be retested[PK90]. This retesting must be done since the inherited components are being used in a new context and there some unexpected dependencies may be affecting

```
class C {
  public:
    int v;
    void J() { v=0; ...; }
    ...
};


class D : public C {
  public:
    void K() { v=1; ...; }
};
```

FIGURE E.3. Example for antidecomposition axiom.

them in this new environment. Once again we shall use an example from Perry and Kaiser[PK90], shown in figure E.3. In this example, class D is a derived class of class C and is inheriting a data member v from it. This member v is initialized by a method from the base class C and a method from the derived class D. The *antidecomposition* axiom tells us that method J of the base class that uses data member v must be retested again when a derived class of C is created or modified.

Our strategy also satisfies this axiom. If v is a `public` or `protected` data member of class C, then it can be used by any member function of the derived class. If we assume it is so, a method K of derived class D can use it. Using our strategy, when base class C was tested, method J was tested in relationship to other member functions of the class. Now, since a member function of the derived class D is using the same data member, it will be retested in relationship to all member functions sharing its usage. Thus member functions J and K will be tested in the derived class environment, and hence J is retested.

E.2.4 Anticomposition

There exists programs P and Q, and test set T, such that T is adequate for P, and the set of vectors of values that variables can assume on entrance to Q for inputs in T is adequate for Q, but T is not adequate for $P; Q$.

This axiom points out that adequately testing all the parts of a program in isolation does not ensure that the whole program has been adequately tested. Putting two components togethermay result in some unexpected interaction that cannot arise in isolation. This axiom may in fact be the motivating force behind testing individual classes as units. Testing each method of a class in isolation does not ensure that class has been tested adequately. According to Doug Lea[DLF93], "Operations may behave differently when objects are in different logical states." Therefore, individually testing each operation is not sufficient to validate a class. Our testing strategy essentially tests this interaction of methods.

References

[AE92]   W.W. Agresti and W.M. Evanco. Projecting Software Defects from Analyzing Ada Designs. *IEEE Transactions on Software Engineering*, 18(11), Nov. 1992.

[AF94]   T.R. Arnold and W.A. Fuson. Testing "In a Perfect World". *Communications of the ACM*, 37(3):78–86, Sep. 1994.

[Amb94]   S. Ambler. Use-Case Scenario Testing. *Software Development*, 3(6):53–61, Jul. 1994.

[Amb96]   S. Ambler. Testing Objects. *Software Development*, 4(8):55–62, Aug. 1996.

[Amb97]   S.W. Ambler. *Building Object Applications That Work*. SIGS Books, 1997.

[ANS91]   ANSI/IEEE. *An American National Standard IEEE Glossary of Software Engineering Terminology Standard 610.12-1990*. IEEE, 1991.

[APH97]   R. Alexander, P. Payne, and C. Hutchinson. Design for Testability for Object-Oriented Software. *Object Magazine*, Jul. 1997.

[ARE96]   T. Ashok, K. Rangaraajan, and P. Eswar. Retesting C++ Classes. In *Ninth International Software Quality Week*, San Francisco, May 1996. Software Research Inc.

[Bak94]   B. Baksaas. Computer-Aided Software Testing. *Dr. Dobb's Journal*, pages 36–38, Feb. 1994.

[Bas93]   I. Bashir. *A Semiexhaustive Testing Technique For C++ Classes Based on Intermember Relationship*. PhD thesis, Syracuse University, Dec. 1993.

[BAS94]   S. Barbey, M. Ammann, and A. Strohmeier. Open Issues in Testing Object-Oriented Software. In *Proceedings of the European Con-*

ference on Software Quality (ECSQ '94), pages 257–267, Basel, Switzerland, 1994.

[Bas96]   I. Bashir. CARE Volume Testing. LCI International internal document, 1996.

[Bas99]   I. Bashir. Object-Oriented Software Testing: Life-Cycle Perspectives. In *Sixteenth International Conference and Exposition on Testing Computer Software*, Bethasda, MD, Jun. 1999. Frontier Technologies, Inc., and USPDI.

[Bau93]   B. Bauerie. Position Statement. OOPSLA'93 Workshop on Testing Object-Oriented Software, Oct. 1993.

[BB91]   I. Bashir and U. Bellur. A Class Flattening Tool. In *C++-at-Work Conference*, Nov. 1991.

[BBP96]   S. Barbey, D. Buchs, and C. Peraire. A Theory of Specification-Based Testing for Object-Oriented Software. In *Proceedings of the second European Dependable Computing Conference (EDCC-2)*, pages 303–320, Taormina, Italy, 1996.

[BC96]   F. Belli and R. Crisan. Towards Automation of Checklist-Based Code Reviews. In *The Seventh International Symposium on Software Reliability Engineering*. IEEE, Oct./Nov. 1996.

[Bec94]   K. Beck. Simple Smalltalk Testing. *The Smalltalk Report*, 4(2):16–18, Oct. 1994.

[Bei90]   B. Beizer. *Software Testing Techniques*. Van Nostrand Reinhold, 1990.

[Bei95]   B. Beizer. *Black Box Testing*. John Wiley & Sons, 1995.

[Ben82]   J.L. Bently. *Writing Efficient Programs*. Prentice Hall, 1982.

[Ber88]   M. Bertrand. *Object-oriented Software Construction*. Prentice Hall, 1988.

[Ber92a]   E.V. Berard. *Essays on Object-Oriented Software Engineering*, volume I. Prentice Hall, 1992.

[Ber92b]   E.V. Berard. Testing of Object-Oriented Software. ACM Seminar, Nov. 1992.

[BG93]   I. Bashir and A.L. Goel. Object-Oriented Metrics and Testing. In *Proceedings of the Fifteenth Minnowbrook Workshop on Software Engineering*, pages 1–9, Syracuse, New York, Jul. 1993. The Center for Advanced Technology in Computer Applications and Software Engineering(CASE), Syracuse University.

[BG94]   I. Bashir and A.L. Goel. Testing C++ Classes. In *International Conference on Software Testing, Reliability, and Quality Assurance*. IEEE, Dec. 1994.

[BG95]   I. Bashir and A.L. Goel. Measurement of Object-Oriented Software. In *Proceedings of the Seventeenth Minnowbrook Workshop on Software Engineering*, Syracuse, New York, Jul. 1995. The Center for Advanced Technology in Computer Applications and Software Engineering(CASE), Syracuse University.

[BG97]   I. Bashir and A.L. Goel. Metrics Guided Testing of Object-Oriented Software. In *Tenth International Software Quality Week*, San Francisco, May 1997. Software Research Inc.

[Bie91]   J.M. Bieman. Deriving Measures of Software Reuse in Object Oriented Systems. Technical Report CS-91-112, Colorado State University, Jul. 1991.

[Bil93]   S.C. Bilow. Guest editorial. *Journal of Object-Oriented Programming*, Jan. 1993.

[Bin94a]   R. Binder. Design for Testability with Object-Oriented Systems. *Communications of the ACM*, 37(7):87–101, Sep. 1994.

[Bin94b]   R. Binder. Testing Object-Oriented Software. *American Programmer*, 7(4):22–28, Apr. 1994.

[Bin95a]   R. Binder. State-Based Testing. *Object Magazine*, 5(4):75–78, Jul.-Aug. 1995.

[Bin95b]   R. Binder. State-based Testing: Sneak paths and Conditional Transitions. *Object Magazine*, 5(6):87–89, Nov.-Dec. 1995.

[Bin95c]   R. Binder. Testing Objects: Myth and Reality. *Object Magazine*, 5(2):73–75, May 1995.

[Bin95d]   R. Binder. The FREE-flow Graph: Implementation-Based Testing of Objects Using State-Determined Flows. In *Eighth International Software Quality Week*, San Francisco, May 1995. Software Research Inc.

[Bin95e]   R. Binder. Trends in Testing Object-Oriented Software. *Object Magazine*, 28(10):68–69, Oct. 1995.

[Bin96a]   R. Binder. An Integrated Tool Suite for High-Reliability Object-Oriented Client/Server Systems. In *Ninth International Software Quality Week*, San Francisco, May 1996. Software Research Inc.

[Bin96b]   R. Binder. Bigfoot's Tootsie. *Object Magazine*, 6(4):81–87, Jun. 1996.

[Bin96c]   R. Binder. Modal Testing Strategies for Object-Oriented Software. *Computer*, 29(11):97–99, Nov. 1996.

[Bin96d]   R. Binder. Off-the-Shelf Test Automation for Objects. *Object Magazine*, 6(2):26–30, Apr. 1996.

[Bin96e]   R. Binder. Summertime, and the testin' is easy ... *Object Magazine*, 6(8), Oct. 1996.

[Bin96f]   R. Binder. Testing for Reuse: Libraries and Frameworks. *Object Magazine*, 6(6), Aug. 1996.

[Bin96g]   R. Binder. Testing Object-Oriented Software: A Survey. *Journal of Software Testing, Verification and Reliability*, 1996.

[Bin96h]   R. Binder. Use-cases, Threads, and Relations: The FREE Approach to System Testing. *Object Magazine*, 5(9):73–81, Feb. 1996.

[Bin96i]   R.V. Binder. Testing Object-Oriented Software: A Survey. *Journal of Software Testing, Verification, and Reliability*, 6:125–252, Dec. 1996.

[Bin96j]   R.V. Binder. The FREE Approach to Object-Oriented Testing: An Overview. http://www.rbsc.com/pages/FREE.html, 1996.

[Bin97a]   R. Binder. Automated Java Testing. *Object Magazine*, Jul. 1997.

[Bin97b]   R. Binder. Class Modality and Testing. *Object Magazine*, 6(2), Feb. 1997.

[Bin97c]   R. Binder. Developing a Test Budget. *Object Magazine*, Jun. 1997.

[Blu92]   B.I. Blum. *Software Engineering: A Holistic View.* Oxford University Press, 1992.

[BM79]   R.S. Boyer and J.S. Moore. *A Computational Logic*. New York: Academic Press, 1979.

[BM85]   R.S. Boyer and J.S. Moore. An Overview of Automated Reasoning and Related Fields. *Journal of Automated Reasoning*, 1(1):17–23, 1985.

[BMP96]   A. Bertolino, R. Mirandola, and E. Peciola. A Case Study In Branch Testing Automation. In S. Bologan and G. Bucci, editors, *Third International Conference on Achieving Quality in Software*, pages 369–380, London, 1996. Chapman and Hall.

[Boe84]   B.W. Boehm. Verifying and Validating Software Requirements and Design Specifications. *IEEE Software*, 1(1):75–88, Jan. 1984.

[Boe88]   B.W. Boehm. A Spiral Model of Software Development and Enhancement. *IEEE Computer*, pages 61–72, May 1988.

[Boi97]   J. Boisvert. OO Testing in the Ericsson Pilot Project. *Object Magazine*, Jul. 1997.

[Boo86]   G. Booch. Object-Oriented Development. *IEEE Transactions on Software Engineering*, SE-12(2):211–221, Feb. 1986.

[Boo91]   G. Booch. *Object Oriented Design with Applications*. Benjamin/Cummings, 1991.

[Boo94]   G. Booch. *Object Oriented Analysis And Design With Applications*. Benjamin/Cummings, 2nd edition, 1994.

[Boo96]   G. Booch. *Object Solutions*. Addison-Wesley, 2nd edition, 1996.

[Bos96]   O. Bosman. Testing and Iterative Development: Adapting the Booch Method. In *Thirteenth International Conference and Exposition on Testing Computer Software*, pages 1–10, Silver Spring, MD., Jun. 1996. USPDI.

[BP95]   R. Bellinzona and B. Pernici. Reusing Specifications in OO Applications. *IEEE Software*, 12(2), Mar. 1995.

[BQF95]   J.R. Brown, L.H. Quandt, and M.C. Fuher. Integration Strategies for OO Software. In *STAR '95*, pages 55–76, Jacksonville, FL, May 1995. Software Quality Engineering.

[BR87]   T. Biggerstaff and C. Richter. Reusability, Framework, Assessment, and Directions. *IEEE Software*, pages 41–49, Mar. 1987.

[Bri95]   J.W. Britt. A Study of the Effectiveness of Selected Testing Techniques in Object-Oriented Programs. Master's thesis, Mississippi State University, 1995.

[Bro87]   F.P. Brooks. No Silver Bullet. *IEEE Computer*, Apr. 1987.

[Buc81]   F.O. Buck. Indicators of Quality Inspections. Technical Report TR21.802, IBM, Sep. 1981.

[Bud91]   T. Budd. *An Introduction to Object-Oriented Programming*. Addison-Wesley, 1991.

[CA88]   D.N. Card and W.W. Agresti. Measuring Software Design Complexity. *Journal of Systems and Software*, 8:185–197, Mar. 1988.

[Car95]   T.A. Cargill. Short Tour Testing. *C++ Report*, 7(2), Feb. 1995.

[CCA86]   D.N. Card, V.E. Church, and W.W. Agresti. An Empirical Study of Software Design Practices. *IEEE Transactions on Software Engineering*, SE-12:264–271, Feb. 1986.

[CCHJ94]   N.P. Capper, R.J. Colgate, J.C. Hunter, and M.F. James. The Impact of Object-Oriented Technology on Software Quality. *IBM Systems Journal*, 33(1):131–157, 1994.

[CFL93]   D. Champeaux, P. Faure, and D. Lea. *Object Oriented Analysis and Design*. Addison-Wesley, 1993.

[Che96]   Y. Chernak. A Statistical Approach to the Inspection Checklist Formal Synthesis and Improvement. *IEEE Transactions On Software Engineering*, 22(12):866–874, Dec. 1996.

[CHK+95]   M.C. Campbell, D.K. Hinds, A.V. Kapetanakis, D.S. Levin, S.J. McFarland, D.J. Miller, and J.S. Southworth. Object-Oriented Perspective on Software System Testing in a Distributed Environment. *Hewlett-Packard Journal*, 46(6), Dec. 1995.

[Chu89]   C.-M. Chung. Object-Oriented Concurrent Programming from Testing View. In *National Computer Symposium*, pages 555–565, 1989.

[Chu95]   I.S. Chung. Methods of Comparing Test Criteria for Object-Oriented Programs Based on Subsumption, Power Relation and Test Reusability. *Journal of Korea Information Science Society*, 22(5):693–704, May 1995.

[CK91]   S.R. Chidamber and C.F. Kemerer. Towards a Metrics Suite for Object Oriented Design. In *OOPSLA*, pages 197–211, 1991.

[CK93]   S.R. Chidamber and C.F. Kemerer. A Metrics Suite for Object Oriented Design. Working Paper 249, M.I.T. Sloan School of Management, Feb 1993.

[CK97]   M-H. Chen and H.M. Kao. Investigating the Relationship Between Class Testing and the Reliability of Object-Oriented Programs. In *Eighth International Symposium on Software Reliability Engineering(ISSRE '97)*, Alburquerque, NM, Nov. 1997. IEEE Computer Society Technical Council on Software Engineering.

[CKH+96]   K-N. Chang, D. Kung, P. Hsia, Y. Toyoshima, and C. Chen. Object-Oriented Data Flow Testing. In *Thirteenth International Conference and Exposition on Testing Computer Software*, pages 97–100, Silver Spring, MD, Jun. 1996. USPDI.

[CL92]   C.-M. Chung and M.-C. Lee. Object-Oriented Programming Testing Methodology. In *Fourth International Conference on Software Engineering and Knowledge Engineering*, pages 378–385. IEEE Computer Society Press, Jun. 1992.

[CL94]   C.M. Chung and M.C. Lee. Object-Oriented Programming Testing Methodology. *International Journal of Mini and Microcomputers*, 16(2):73–81, 1994.

[CLW94]   C.-M. Chung, M.-C. Lee, and C.-C. Wang. Inheritance Testing for OO Programming by Transitive Closure Strategies. *Advances in Modeling and Analysis*, 31(2):57–64, 1994. AMSE Press.

[CM90]   T.J. Cheatham and L. Mellinger. Testing Object-Oriented Systems. In *Eighteenth ACM Annual Computer Science Conference*, pages 161–165, 1990.

[CMLK96a]   I.S. Chung, M. Munro, W.K. Lee, and Y.R. Kwon. Applying Conventional Testing Techniques for Class Testing. In *Proceedings of the Twentieth Annual International Computer Software & Applica-*

tions Conference (COMPSAC '96), Seoul, Korea, pages 447–454. IEEE Computer Society, Korea Information Science Society, Aug. 21-23 1996.

[CMLK96b] I.S. Chung, M. Munro, W.K. Lee, and Y.R. Kwon. Applying Conventional Testing Techniques for Class Testing. In *Proceedings The Twentieth Annual International Computer Software & Applications Conference (COMPSAC '96), Seoul, Korea*, pages 447–454. The IEEE Computer Society, Korea Information Science Society, Aug 21-23 1996.

[CN91] B.J. Cox and A.J. Novobilski. *Object-Oriented Programming An Evolutionary Approach*. Addison-Wesley, 1991.

[Cop92] J.O. Coplien. *Advanced C++ Programming Styles and Idioms*. Addison Wesley, 1992.

[Cor95] Reliable Software Technologies Corporation. Testability of Object-Oriented Systems. Technical Report NIST GCR 95-675, National Institute of Standards and Technology, Computer System Laboratory, Gaithersburg, MD 20899, 1995.

[Cra93] G.L. Craig. Personal communication, Nov. 1993.

[Cro79] P. Crosby. *Quality Is Free*. McGraw-Hill, 1979.

[CS93] B.P. Chao and D.M. Smith. Applying Software Testing Practices to an Object-Oriented Software Development. In *Addendum to the Proceedings OOPSLA '93*, pages 49–52, Washington, DC, Sep. 26 - Oct. 1 1993.

[CS94] B.P. Chao and D.M. Smith. Applying Software Testing Practices to an Object-Oriented Software Development. *OOPS Messenger*, 5(2), Apr. 1994.

[CS96] M.A. Cusumano and R.W. Selby. *Microsoft Secrets*. HarperCollins, 1996. First published in the United States by The Free Press 1995.

[CS97] M.A. Cusumano and R.W. Selby. How Microsoft Builds Software. *Communications of the ACM*, 40(6):53–61, Jun. 1997.

[CSM95] M.J. Chonoles, J.A. Stuart, and P.J. Magrogan. OO Systems from a Quality Perspective. *Report on Object Analysis and Design (ROAD)*, 2(4):46–55, Nov.-Dec. 1995.

[DE82] R.B. Dannenberg and G.W. Ernst. Formal Program Verification Using Symbolic Execution. *IEEE Transactions on Software Engineering*, SE-8:43–52, Jan. 1982.

[DeM82] T. DeMarco. *Controlling Software Projects*. Yourdon Press, 1982.

[DF91] R.K. Doong and P.G. Frankl. Case Studies in Testing Object-Oriented Programs. In *The Testing, Analysis and Verification Symposium*, pages 165–177, New York, 1991. ACM Inc.

[DF94] R.K. Doong and P.G. Frankl. The ASTOOT Approach to Testing Object-Oriented Programs. *ACM Transactions on Software Engineering and Methodology*, 3(4):101–130, Apr. 1994.

[DG94] D.S. Dunaway and E. Gillan. Applying Object-Oriented Design Principles to Developing a Test Strategy. In *Proceedings of the Eleventh International Conference and Exposition on Testing Computer Software*, pages 341–368. ASQC and STSC, Jun. 1994.

[DLF93] D. DeChampeaux, D. Lea, and P. Faure. *Object-Oriented Systems Development*. Addison-Wesley, 1993.

[DLJ94]   R.J. D'Souza and R.J. LeBlanc Jr. Class Testing by Examining Pointers. *Journal of Object-Oriented Programming*, pages 33–39, Jul.-Aug. 1994.

[Doo93]   R.K. Doong. *An Approach To Testing Object-Oriented Programs.* PhD thesis, Polytechnic University, New York, 1993.

[Dor93]   M. Dorman. Unit Testing of C++ Objects. In *EuroSTAR 93*, pages 71–101. SQE Inc., Oct. 1993.

[Dus99]   E. Dustin. Moving from Conventional to Object-Oriented Testing. In *International Conference On Software Testing Analysis and Review (STAR '99 East)*, Orlando, FL, May 1999. Software Quality Engineering.

[Dye87]   M. Dyer. A Formal Approach to Software Error Removal. *Journal of Systems and Software*, pages 109–114, 1987.

[EKOS92a]   W. Eder, G. Kappel, J. Overbeck, and M. Schrefl. Object-Oriented Analysis and Design - A Case Study. In R. Mittermeir, editor, *Proceedings of the Seventh Joint Austrian and Hungarian Conference Shifting Paradigms in Software Engineering, SPSE '92*. Austrian Computer Society, John von Neumann Society for Computing Sciences, Springer-Verlag, 1992.

[EKOS92b]   W. Eder, G. Kappel, J. Overbeck, and M. Schrefl. Reengineering a Non Object-Oriented System with Object-Oriented Methods. Forschungsbericht MooD 92/04, Institut für Informationssysteme, TU Wien, Apr. 1992.

[ES90]   M.A. Ellis and B. Stroustrup. *The Annotated C++ Reference Manual*. Addison-Wesley, 1990.

[Fag76]   M.E. Fagan. Design and Code Inspections to Reduce Errors in Program Development. *IBM Systems Journal*, 15(3):219–248, Mar. 1976.

[Fag86]   M.E. Fagan. Advances in Software Inspections. *IEEE Transactions on Software Engineering*, SE-12(7):744–751, Jul. 1986.

[Fai85]   R. Fairley. *Software Engineering Concepts*. McGraw-Hill, 1985.

[FD90]   P.G. Frankl and R. Doong. Tools for Testing Object-Oriented Programs. In *Proceedings of the Pacific Northwest Conference on Software Quality*, pages 309–324, 1990.

[FD91]   P.G. Frankl and R.K. Doong. Testing Object-Oriented Programs with ASTOOT. In *Software Quality Week*, San Francisco, CA, 1991. Software Research Inc.

[FFN91]   W.B. Frakes, C.J. Fox, and B.A. Nejmeh. *Software Engineering in the UNIX/C Environment*. Prentice Hall, 1991.

[FHK+97]   F. Ferguson, W.S. Humphrey, S. Khajenoori, S. Macke, and A. Matvya. Results of Applying the Personal Software Process. *IEEE Computer*, 30(5):24–32, May 1997.

[Fie89]   S.P. Fiedler. Object-Oriented Unit Testing. *Hewlett-Packard Journal*, pages 69–74, Apr. 1989.

[Fir93]   D.G. Firesmith. Testing Object-Oriented Software. In *Eleventh International Conference on Technology of Object-Oriented Languages and Systems (TOOLS USA '93)*, pages 407–426. Prentice Hall, 1993.

[Fir95]   D.G. Firesmith. Object-Oriented Regression Testing. *Report on Object Analysis and Design (ROAD)*, 1(5):42–45, Jan/Feb. 1995.

[Fir96]   D.G. Firesmith. Pattern Language for Testing Object-Oriented Software. *Object Magazine*, 5(9):32–38, Jan. 1996.

[FLN91]   W.B. Frakes, D.J. Lubinsky, and D.N. Neal. Experimental Evaluation of a Test Coverage Analyzer for C and C++. *Journal of Systems and Software*, pages 135–139, 1991.

[FR90]   P. Fowler and S. Rifkin. Software Engineering Process Group Guide. Technical Report CM/SEI-90-TR-24, Software Engineering Institute, Sep. 1990.

[Fra91]   W.B. Frakes. Experimental Evaluation of a Test Coverage Analyzer for C and C++. *Journal of Systems and Software*, 16, 1991.

[Fre91]   R.S. Freedman. Testability of Software Components. *IEEE Transactions on Software Engineering*, 17(6):553–564, Jun. 1991.

[FW82]   D.P. Freedman and G.M. Weinberg. *Handbook of Walkthroughs, Inspections, and Technical Reviews*. Little,Brown, 1982.

[FW86]   P.G. Frankl and E.J. Weyuker. Data Flow Testing in the Presence of Unexecutable Paths. In *Workshop on Software Testing*, pages 4–13, Banff, Canada, Jul. 1986.

[GDT93]   J.A. Graham, A.C.T. Drakeford, and C.D. Turner. The Verification, Validation and Testing of Object-Oriented Systems. *BT Technology Journal*, 11(3):79–88, 1993.

[Gea77]   M. Gordon and et al. A Metalanguage For Interactive Proof In LCF. Technical Report CSR-16-77, Department of Computer Science, Univ. of Edinburgh, 1977.

[Gil94]   T. Giltinan. Leveraging Inheritance to Test Objects. In *STAR '94*, pages 361–372, Jacksonville, FL, May 1994. Software Quality Engineering.

[GKH$^+$95] J.Z. Gao, D. Kung, P. Hsia, Y. Toyoshima, and C. Chen. Object State Testing For Object-Oriented Programs. In *Proceedings of the Nineteenth Annual International Computer Software & Applications Conference (COMPSAC '95)*, pages 232–238, Dallas, TX, Aug. 9-11 1995. IEEE Computer Society.

[GKS92]   M. Ghiassi, M. Ketabchi, and K. Sadeghi. Integrated Software Testing System Based on an Object-Oriented DBMS. In *Proceedings of the Twentyfifth Annual Hawaii International Conference on System Sciences (HICSS-25)*. IEEE Press, 1992.

[GO79]   A.L. Goel and K. Okumoto. A Time-Dependent Error Detection Model for Software Reliability and Other Performance Measures. *IEEE Transactions on Reliability*, pages 206–211, Aug. 1979.

[Goo82]   D.I. Good. The Proof Of A Distributed System In Gypsy. Technical Report ICSCA-CMP-30, Institute of Computer Science and Computer Application, University of Texas at Austin, 1982.

[GR95]   A. Goldberg and K.S. Rubin. *Succeeding with Objects: Decision Frameworks for Project Management*. Addison-Wesley, 1995.

[Gra94]   I. Graham. *Object-Oriented Methods*. Addison-Wesley, 2nd edition, 1994.

[Gra95]   I. Graham. *Migrating to Object Technology*. Addison-Wesley, 1995.

[Har93]   M.J. Harrold. Program-Based Testing of Object-Oriented Programs, Oct. 1993. OOPSLA '93 Workshop on Testing Object-Oriented Software.

[Hay94]   J.H. Hayes. Testing of Object-Oriented Programming Systems (OOPS): a Fault-Based Approach. In E. Bertino and S. Urban, editors, *Object-Oriented Methodologies and Systems*. Springer-Verlag, 1994.

[HD93]   A. Hossain and R. Dahiya. Estimating the Parameters of a Non-Homogeneous Poisson-Process Model of Software Reliability. *IEEE Transactions on Reliability*, pages 604–612, Dec. 1993.

[Heg89]   W.A. Hegazy. *The Requirements of Testing a Class of Reusable Software Modules*. PhD thesis, Ohio State University, 1989.

[Het88]   B. Hetzel. *The Complete Guide to Software Testing*. John Wiley & Sons, 2nd edition, 1988.

[HF94]   D. Hoffman and X. Fang. Testing the C Set++ Collection Class Library. In *CASCON 94*, Toronto, Canada, 1994. IBM Center for Advanced Studies.

[HJJ93]   B. Hinke, V. Jones, and R.E. Johnson. Debugging Objects. *The Smalltalk Report*, 2(9), Jul./Aug. 1993.

[HK97]   P. Hsia and D. Kung. An Object-Oriented Testing and Maintenance Environment. In *Proceedings of the International Conference on Software Engineering (ICSE'97)*, pages 608–609, Boston, 1997. ACM.

[HKC95]   H.S. Hong, Y.R. Kwon, and S.D. Cha. Testing of Object-Oriented Programs Based on Finite State Machines. In *Asia-Pacific Software Engineering Conference (ASPEC)'95*, Brisbane, Australia, Dec. 1995.

[HM84]   E. Horowitz and J.B. Munson. An Expansive View of Reusable Software. *IEEE Transactions on Software Engineering*, SE-10(5):477–487, Sep. 1984.

[HMF92]   M.J. Harrold, J.D. McGregor, and K.J. Fitzpatrick. Incremental Testing of Object-Oriented Class Structures. In *Fourteenth International Conference on Software Engineering*. ACM Inc., 1992.

[Hob95]   J. Hobart. Principles of Good GUI Design. *Unix Review*, 13(10):37–46, Sep. 1995.

[Hof89]   D.M. Hoffman. Hardware Testing and Software ICs. In *Proceedings of the Pacific NorthWest Conference on Software Quality*, pages 234–244, Sep. 1989.

[HR94]   M.J. Harrold and G. Rothermel. Performing Data Flow Testing on Classes. In *Second ACM SIGSOFT Symposium on Foundations of Software Engineering*, pages 154–163. ACM Inc., 1994.

[HR95]   M.J. Harrold and G. Rothermel. Structural Testing of Object-Oriented Classes. In *Eighth Annual Software Quality Week*, San Francisco, 1995. Software Research Inc.

[HRHH97] T. Hammer, L. Rosenberg, L. Huffman, and L. Hyatt. Measuring Requirements Testing: Experience Report. In *Proceedings of International Conference on Software Engineering*, pages 372–379, Boston, May 1997. ACM.

[HS93a]   D. Hoffman and P. Strooper. A Case Study In Class Testing. In *CASCON 93*, pages 472–482, Toronto, Oct. 1993. IBM Toronto Lab.

[HS93b]   D. Hoffman and P. Strooper. Graph-Based Class Testing. In *Seventh Australian Software Engineering Conference*, pages 85–91. IREE, Sep./Oct. 1993.

[HS95a]   D. Hoffman and P. Strooper. ClassBench: A Framework For Class Testing. In *8th Annual Software Quality Week*, San Francisco, CA., May 1995. Software Research Inc.

[HS95b]   D. Hoffman and P. Strooper. The Testgraph Methodology: Automated Testing of Collection Classes. *Journal of Object-Oriented Programming*, 8(7), Nov./Dec. 1995.

[HS96]   M. Hughes and D. Stotts. Daistish: Systematic Algebraic Testing for OO Programs in the Presence of Side-effects. In S.J. Zeil, editor, *Proceedings of the 1996 International Symposium on Software Testing and Analysis(ISSTA)*, pages 53–61, San Diego, Jan. 8-10 1996. Association for Computing Machinery.

[HSE90]   B. Henderson-Sellers and J.M. Edwards. The Object-Oriented Systems Lifecycle. *Communications of the ACM*, 33(9):142–159, Sep. 1990.

[HSS94]   D. Hoffman, J. Smillie, and A. Stroper. Automated Class Testing: Methods and Experience. In *First Asia-Pacific Software Engineering Conference*, pages 163–171, Washington,DC., 1994. IEEE Computer Society.

[HT93]   P. Harmon and D. Taylor. *Objects in Action: Commercial Applications of Object-Oriented Technologies*. Addison-Wesley, 1993.

[Hum96]   W.S. Humphrey. Using A Defined and Measured Personal Software Process. *IEEE Software*, pages 77–88, May 1996.

[Hun95a]   N. Hunt. Automatically Tracking Test Case Execution. *Journal of Object-Oriented Programming*, 8(7):22–27, Nov./Dec. 1995.

[Hun95b]   N. Hunt. C++ Boundary Conditions and Edge Cases. *Journal of Object-Oriented Programming*, pages 25–29, May 1995.

[Hun96a]   N. Hunt. Performance Testing C++ Code. *Journal of Object-Oriented Programming*, pages 22–25, Jan. 1996.

[Hun96b]   N. Hunt. Unit Testing. *Journal of Object-Oriented Programming*, pages 18–23, Feb. 1996.

[HW94]   J. Hurst and R. Willhoft. The Use of Coherence Checking for Testing Object-Oriented Code. In *IBM International Conference on Object Technology*. IBM, Jun. 1994.

[HY88]   Y. Honda and A. Yonezawa. Debugging Concurrent Systems Based on Object Groups. In G. Gjessing and K. Nygaard, editors, *Proceedings of the European Conference on Object-Oriented Programming (ECOOP '88), Lecture Notes on Computer Science*, pages 267–282, New York, 1988. Springer-Verlag.

[IEE83]   ANSI IEEE. *An American National Standard IEEE Glossary of Software Engineering Terminology*. IEEE, 1983.

[ILJ75]   S. Igarashi, R.L. London, and D.C. Juckham. Automatic Program Verification I: A Logical Basis and Its Implementation. *Acta Inform.*, 4(1):145–182, 1975.

[Inc97]   Software Research Inc. Software Quality HotList. http://www.soft.com/Institute/HotList, Jan. 1997.

[Jal87]   P. Jalote. Synthesizing Implementations of Abstract Data Types from Axiomatic Specification. *Software-Practice and Experience*, 17(11):847–858, Nov. 1987.

[Jal89]   P. Jalote. Testing the Completeness of Specification. *IEEE Transactions on Software Engineering*, 15(5):526–531, May 1989.

[Jal91]   P. Jalote. *An Integrated Approach to Software Engineering*. Springer-Verlag, 1991.

[Jal92]   P. Jalote. Specification and Testing of Abstract Data Types. *Computer Language*, 17(1):75–82, 1992.

[JC88]   P. Jalote and D. Caballero. Automated Testcase Generation for Data Abstraction. In *Twelfth Annual International Computer Software and Applications Conference*, pages 205–209. IEEE Computer Society Press, Nov. 1988.

[JCJO92]   I. Jacobson, M. Christenson, P. Jonson, and G. Overgaard. *Object-Oriented Software Engineering: A Use Case Driven Approach* . ACM Press/Addison-Wesley, New York, 1992.

[JE94]   P.C. Jorgensen and Erickson.C. Object-Oriented Integration Testing. *Communications of the ACM*, 37(9):30–38, Sep. 1994.

[Jia93]   X. Jia. Model-Based Formal Specification Directed Testing of Abstract Data Types. In *The Seventeenth Annual International Computer Software and Applications Conference*, pages 360–366. IEEE Computer Society Press, Nov. 1993.

[JKNZ94a]   P. Juttner, S. Kolb, U. Naumann, and P. Zimmerer. A Complete Test Process in Object-Oriented Software Development. In *Seventh Annual Software Quality Week*, San Francisco, May 1994. Software Research Inc.

[JKNZ94b]   P. Juttner, S. Kolb, U. Naumann, and P. Zimmerer. Experiences In Testing Object-Oriented Software. In *Eleventh International Conference on Testing Computer Software*, Washington, DC, Jun. 1994. USPDI.

[JKZ94]   P. Juttner, S. Kolb, and P. Zimmerer. Integration and Testing of Object-Oriented Software. In *EuroSTAR 94*, pages 71–101, Jacksonville, FL, Oct. 1994. SQE Inc.

[Jon86]   C. Jones. *Programming Productivity*. McGraw-Hill, 1986.

[Jon94]   C. Jones. *Assessment and Control of Software Risks*. Prentice Hall, 1994.

[Jon95]   A.M. Jonassen. Managing Unit and Integration Testing of a Large Object-Oriented System. In *Eighth Annual Software Quality Week*, San Francisco, May 1995. Software Research Inc.

[Jor95]   P.C. Jorgenson. *Software Testing: A Craftman's Approach*. CRC Press, 1995.

[Kan92]   S.H. Kan. *Metrics and Models in Software Quality Engineering*. Addison-Wesley, 1992.

[Kec91]   D. Kececioglu. *Reliability Engineering Handbook*, volume 2. Prentice Hall, Englewood Cliffs, NJ, 1991.

[Kep94]   L.R. Kepple. The Black Art of GUI Testing. *Dr. Dobb's Journal*, Feb. 1994.

[KGH+93]   D. Kung, J. Gao, P. Hsia, J. Lin, and Y. Toyoshima. Design Recovery for Software Testing of Object-Oriented Programs. In *Proceedings Working Conference on Reverse Engineering*, pages 202–211, Baltimore, 1993.

[KGH+94]   D. Kung, J. Gao, P. Hsia, F. Wen, Y. Toyoshima, and C. Chen. Change Impact Identification in Object-Oriented Software Maintenance. In *International Computer on Software Maintenance*, pages 202–211. IEEE Computer Society Press, 1994.

[KGH+95a]   D. Kung, J. Gao, P. Hsia, Y. Toyoshima, C. Chen, Y.-S. Kim, and Y.-K. Song. Developing and Object-Oriented Software Testing and Maintenance Environment. *Communications of the ACM*, 38(10):75–87, Oct. 1995.

[KGH+95b]   D. Kung, J.Z. Gao, P. Hsia, Y. Toyoshima, and C. Chen. A Test Strategy for Object-Oriented Programs. In *Proceedings of the Nineteenth Annual International Computer Software & Applications Conference (COMPSAC '95), Dallas, Texas*, pages 239–244. The IEEE Computer Society, Aug. 9-11 1995.

[KGH+95c]   D.C. Kung, J. Gao, P. Hsia, J. Lin, and Y. Toyoshima. Class firewall, test order, and regression testing of object-oriented programs. *Journal of Object-Oriented Programming*, pages 51–66, May 1995.

[KGHC96]   D. Kung, J. Gao, P. Hsia, and C. Chen. On Regression Testing of Object-Oriented Programs. *Journal Of Systems and Software*, 32(1), Jan. 1996.

[Kir94]   S. Kirani. *Specification and Verification of Object-Oriented Programs*. PhD thesis, University of Minnesota, 1994.

[KL94]   L.M. Keszenheimer and K.J. Lieberherr. Incremental Testing of Adaptive Software. Technical Report NU-CSS-94-22, Northeastern University, Boston, Nov. 1994.

[KL95]   L.M. Keszenheimer and K.J. Lieberherr. Testing Adaptive Software During Class Evolution. Technical Report NU-CSS-95-xx, Northeastern University, Boston, MA., Jan. 1995.

[Kli92]   E. Klimas. Quality Assurance Issues for Smalltalk-based Applications. *The Smalltalk Report*, 1(9):3–7, Jul./Aug. 1992.

[KLV+96]   D. Kung, Y. Lu, N. Venugopalan, P. Hsia, Y. Toyoshima, C. Chen, and J. Gao. Object State Testing and Fault Analysis for Reliable Software Systems. In *Proceedings of the Seventh International Symposium on Software Reliability Engineering*, New York, 1996.

[KM93]   J.C. Knight and E.A. Myers. An Improved Inspection Technique. *Communications of the ACM*, 36(11):51–61, Nov. 1993.

[Koc]   G.R. Koch. Maturity Assessments: The BOOTSTRAP Approach. http://stfc.comp.polyu.edu.hk/library/html/bootstrap.html.

[KOS92]   G. Kappel, J. Overbeck, and M. Schrefl. A Process Model for Object-Oriented Development. In *Workshop on Object-Oriented Software Development Process at ECOOP '92*, Utrecht(Netherlands), Jun. 1992.

[KPG95]   M.D. Konrad, M.C. Paulk, and A.W. Graydon. An Overview of SPICE's Model for Process Management. In *Proceedings of the Fifth International Conference on Software Quality*, pages 291–301, Austin, Texas, Oct. 23-26 1995.

[KSG+94]   D. Kung, N. Suchak, J. Gao, P. Hsia, Y. Toyoshima, and C. Chen. On Object State Testing. In *Eighteenth Annual International Computer Software and¿ Applications Conference*, pages 222–227. IEEE Computer Society Press, 1994.

[KT94]   S. Kirani and W.T. Tsai. Method Sequence Specification and Verification of Classes. *Journal of Object-Oriented Programming*, 7(6):28–38, Oct. 1994.

[LC90]   D. Lea and G.L. Craig. CSE691: Class Lectures, Spring 1990. Syracuse University.

[LC92]   A. Lake and C. Cook. A Software Complexity Metric for C++. In *Proceedings of the Fourth Annual Workshop on Software Metrics*, Mar. 1992.

[LDF88]   K.S. Lew, T.S. Dillon, and K.E. Forward. Software Complexity and Its Impact on Software Reliability. *IEEE Transactions on Software Engineering*, 14(11):1645–1655, Nov. 1988.

[Lea91]   G.T. Leavens. Modular Specification and Verification of Object-Oriented Programs. *IEEE Software*, 8(4):72–80, Jul. 1991.

[Lea92]   D. Lea. *User's Guide to the GNU C++ Library*. Free Software Foundation Inc., 1992.

[Lea93]   D. Lea. Personal communication, Nov. 1993.

[Lew91]   T.G. Lewis. *CASE: Computer-Aided Software Engineering*. Van Nostrand Reinhold, 1991.

[LFC94]   J. Lee, M. Feng, and C. Chung. A Structural Testing Method for C++ Programs. In *The Eighteenth Annual International Computer Software and¿ Applications Conference*. IEEE Computer Society Press, 1994.

[Lit81]   B. Littlewood. Stochastic Reliability Growth: A Model for Fault Removal in Computer Programs and Hardware Design. *IEEE Transactions on Reliability*, pages 313–320, Dec. 1981.

[LL89]   C.-C. Lin and R.J. LeVlanc. Event based debugging of object/action programs. *SIGPlan Notices*, 24(1):23–34, Jan. 1989.

[LMR92]   M. Lejter, S. Meyers, and S.P. Reiss. Support for Maintaining Object-Oriented Programs. *IEEE Transactions on Software Engineering*, 18(12):1045–1052, 1992.

[Lov93]   T. Love. *Object Lessons: Lessons Learned in Object-Oriented Development Projects*. SIGS Books, 1993.

[LW95]   G.T Leavens and W.E. Weihl. Specification and Verification of Object-Oriented Programs Using Supertype Abstraction. *Acta Informatica*, 32(8):705–778, 1995.

[Mag96]   M.D. Maggio. A Framework for Distributed Testing. *UNIX Review*, 14(8):43–50, Jul. 1996.

[Maj98]   M. Major. Prioritizing OO Tests Built With Use Cases. In *STAR '98*, Orlando, May 1998. Software Quality Engineering.

[Mar95]   B. Marick. *The Craft of Software Testing*. Prentice Hall, 1995.

[McG94a]   J.D. McGregor. Constructing functional test cases using incrementally derived state machines. In *Eleventh International Conference on Testing Computer Software*, Washington, DC, Jun. 1994. USPDI.

[McG94b]   J.D. McGregor. Functional testing of classes. In *Seventh International Software Quality Week*, San Francisco, May 1994. Software Research Institute.

[McG97a]   J.D. McGregor. A Component Testing Method. *Journal of Object-Oriented Programming*, 10(3), Jun. 1997.

[McG97b]   J.D. McGregor. Component Testing. *Journal of Object-Oriented Programming*, 10(1), Jun. 1997.

[McG97c]   J.D. McGregor. Making Component Testing More Effective. *Journal of Object-Oriented Programming*, 10(4), Jul/Aug. 1997.

[McG97d]   J.D. McGregor. Parallel Architecture For Component Testing. *Journal of Object-Oriented Programming*, 10(2), Jun. 1997.

[Mcg99]   J.D. Mcgregor. Testing Distributed Objects and Components. In *International Conference On Software Testing Analysis and Review (STAR '99 East)*, Orlando, FL, May 1999. Software Quality Engineering.

[MD93a]   J.D. McGregor and D.M. Dyer. A Note on Inheritance and State Machines. *Software Engineering Notes*, 18(4):61–69, Oct. 1993.

[MD93b]   J.D. McGregor and D.M. Dyer. Selecting functional test cases for a class. In *11th Annual Northwest Software Quality Conference*, pages 109–121, Portland, OR., 1993. PNSQC.

[MD97]   P. Middleton and C. Dougan. Grey Box Texting C++ via the Internet. In *Tenth International Software Quality Week*, San Francisco, May 1997. Software Research Inc.

[MDDW94a]   T.J. McCabe, L.A. Dreyer, A.J. Dunn, and A.H. Watson. Testing an Object-Oriented Application. *CASE Outlook*, pages 1–7, Spring 1994.

[MDDW94b]   T.J. McCabe, L.A. Dreyer, A.J. Dunn, and A.H. Watson. Testing an Object-Oriented Application. *Journal of the Quality Assurance Institute*, 8(4):21–27, Oct. 1994.

[Mey87]   B. Meyer. Resuability: The Case for Object-Oriented Design. *IEEE Software*, 4:50–64, Mar. 1987.

[Mey90]   B. Meyer. Lessons from the Design of the Eiffel Libraries. *Communications of the ACM*, 33(9):69–88, Sep. 1990.

[Mey92]   S. Meyers. *Effective C++*. Addison-Wesley Publishing Company, 1992.

[Mey96]   S. Meyers. *More Effective C++*. Addison-Wesley, 1996.

[MG82]   P.R. McMullin and J.D. Gannon. Evaluating a Data Abstraction Testing System Based on Formal Specifications. *Journal of Systems and Software*, 2(2):177–186, 1982.

[MIO87]   J. Musa, A. Iannino, and K. Okumoto. *Software Reliability*. McGraw-Hill, 1987.

[MK94]   J.D. McGregor and T.D. Korson. Integrated Object-Oriented Testing and Development Processes. *Communications Of The ACM*, 37(9):59–77, Sep. 1994.

[MK96]   J.D. McGregor and A. Kare. Parallel Architecture for Component
           Testing of Object-Oriented Software. In *Nineth International Soft-
           ware Quality Week*, San Francisco, May 1996. Software Research
           Institute.

[MN93]   B. Meyer and J. Nerson. *Object-Oriented Applications*. Prentice
           Hall, 1993.

[Mos93]   Daniel J. Mosley. *The Handbook of MIS Application Software
           Testing*. Yourdon Press Computing Series, 1993.

[MS92]   J.D. McGregor and D.A. Sykes. *Object-Oriented Software Devel-
           opment:Engineering Software for Reuse*. Van Nostrand Reinhold,
           1992.

[MTW94]   G.C. Murphy, P. Townsend, and P.S. Wong. Experiences with Clus-
           ter and Class Testing. *Communications of the ACM*, 37(9):39–47,
           Sep. 1994.

[Mus96]   J.D. Musa. Software-Reliability-Engineered Testing. *IEEE Com-
           puter*, 29(11):61–68, Nov. 1996.

[MW94]   T.J. McCabe and A.H. Watson. Combining Comprehension
           and Testing in Object-Oriented Development. *Object Magazine*,
           4(1):63–66, Mar./Apr. 1994.

[Mye79]   G.J. Myers. *The Art of Software Testing*. John Wiley & Sons., 1979.

[Nie96]   J. Nielson. Putting the User in User-Interface Testing. *IEEE
           Software*, pages 89–90, May 1996.

[OI95]   A.J. Offutt and A. Irvine. Testing Object-Oriented Software Us-
           ing the Category-Partition Method. In *TOOLS 17*, pages 293–304,
           1995.

[OKS93]   J. Overbeck, G. Kappel, and M. Schrefl. Introducing Object Tech-
           nology to a Large Organization. In *Workshop on Experiences with
           OO in the Commercial Environment, held in conjunction with
           ECOOP '93*, Kaiserslautern, BRD, Jul 1993.

[Ove92a]   J. Overbeck. Test Activities in Object-Oriented Development.
           In P. Liggesmeyer, H. M. Sneed, and A. Spillner, editors, *Test
           Activities in Object-Oriented Development*, pages 168–177. GI,
           Springer-Verlag, 1992.

[Ove92b]   J. Overbeck. Test Activities in Object-Oriented Development. In
           P. Liggesmeyer, H. M. Sneed, and A. Spillner, editors, *Testen,
           Analysieren und Verifizieren von Software*, pages 168–177. GI,
           Springer-Verlag, 1992.

[Ove92c]   J. Overbeck. Testaktivitäten im objektorientierten Software Leben-
           szyklus. *GI Softwaretechnik Trends*, Feb. 1992.

[Ove93a]   J. Overbeck. Testing Object-Oriented Software: State of the Art
           and Research Directions. In *Proceedings of the First European In-
           ternational Conference on Software Testing, Analysis and Review)*,
           London/UK, Oct. 1993.

[Ove93b]   J. Overbeck. Testing Object-Oriented Software: State of the Art
           and Research Directions. In *Proceedings of the First European In-
           ternational Conference on Software Testing, Analysis and Review*,
           London, Oct. 1993.

[Ove94a]   J. Overbeck. *Integration Testing for Object-Oriented Software*. PhD
           thesis, Vienna University of Technology, 1994.

194   References

[Ove94b]   J. Overbeck. *Integration Testing for Object-Oriented Software*. PhD thesis, Vienna University of Technology, 1994.

[Ove94c]   J. Overbeck. Objektorientierter Integrationstest und Wiederverwendbarkeit. In *5. Treffen des Arbeitskreises "Testen, Analysieren und Verifizieren von Software"*. GI, 1994.

[Ove94d]   J. Overbeck. Testing Generic Classes. In *Proceedings of the Second European International Conference on Software Testing, Analysis and Review*, Brussels, Oct. 1994.

[Ove94e]   J. Overbeck. Testing Generic Classes. In *Proceedings of the Second European International Conference on Software Testing, Analysis and Review*, Brussels, Oct 1994.

[Pay98]   J. Payne. Practical Techniques for Testing Objects. In *STAR '98 West*, San Diego, CA, Oct. 1998. Software Quality Engineering.

[PBC93]   A. Parrish, R. Borie, and D. Cordes. Automated Flowgraph-Based Testing of Object-Oriented Software Modules. *Journal of Systems and Software*, Nov 1993.

[PCB93]   A. Parrish, D. Cordes, and R. Borie. Developmental Testing of Abstract Data Types. In *Seventeenth Annual International Computer Software and Applications Conference*, pages 49–55. IEEE Computer Society, Nov. 1993.

[PCCW93]   M.C. Paulk, B. Curtis, M.B. Chrissis, and C.V. Weber. Capability Maturity Model for Software, Version 1.1. Technical Report CM/SEI-93-TR-24, Software Engineering Institute, 1993.

[PCG94]   A. Parrish, D. Cordes, and M. Govindarajan. Systematic Defect Removal from Object-Oriented Modules. In *Seventh International Software Quality Week*, San Francisco, May 1994. Software Research Institute.

[PDS97]   M.W. Price and S.A. Demurjian Sr. Analyzing and Measuring Reusability in Object-Oriented Designs. In *Proceedings of the OOPSLA '97*, pages 22–33. ACM, 1997.

[Per95]   W. Perry. *Effective Methods for Software Testing*. John Wiley & Sons, Inc., 1995.

[PF95]   S. Porat and P. Fertig. Class Assertions in C++. *Journal of Object-Oriented Programming*, 8(2):30–37, May 1995.

[PG96]   F.A.C. Pinheiro and J.A. Goguen. An Object-Oriented Tool for Tracing Requirements. *IEEE Software*, 13(2), Mar. 1996.

[PK90]   D.E. Perry and G.E. Kaiser. Adequate Testing and Object-Oriented Programming. *Journal of Object-Oriented Programming*, 2:13–19, Jan./Feb. 1990.

[Pos87]   R. Poston. Preventing the most robable errors in requirements. *IEEE Software*, 4(5):81–83, Sep. 1987.

[Pos94]   R.M. Poston. Automated Testing from Object Models. *Communications of the ACM*, 37(9):48–58, Sep. 1994.

[Pre97]   R.S. Pressman. *Software Engineering A Practitioner's Approach*. McGraw-Hill, 1997.

[Pro89]   J.G. Proakis. *Digital Communications*. McGraw-Hill, 2nd edition, 1989.

[PW85]   D.W. Parnas and D.M. Weiss. Active Design Reviews: Principles and Practices. In *Proceedings of ICSE '85*, pages 132–136, Aug 28-30 1985.

[PW91]   J.A. Purchase and R.L. Winder. Debugging Tools for Object-Oriented Programming. *Journal of Object-Oriented Programming*, 4(3):10–27, Jun. 1991.

[PWCC95]   M.C. Paulk, C.V. Weber, B. Curtis, and M.B. Chrissis. *The Capability Maturity Model: Guidelines for Improving the Software Process*. Addison-Wesley, 1995.

[RBP+91]   J. Rumbaugh, M. Blaha, W. Premerlani, F. Eddy, and W. Lorensen. *Object-Oriented Modeling and Design*. Prentice Hall, 1991.

[Ree93]   D.R. Reed. Program Development Using C++. In *C++ World Conference Proceedings*, New York, Apr. 1993. SIGS Conferences.

[Ree94]   D.R. Reed. Building, Testing, and Tuning C++ Programs. In *C++ World Conference Proceedings*, pages 135–137, New York, Jan./Feb. 1994. SIGS Conferences.

[RH94]   G. Rothermel and M.J. Harrold. Selecting Regression Tests for Object-Oriented Software. In Muller,H.A. and Georges,M., editor, *Proceedings of the International Conference on Software Maintenance*, pages 14–25, Victoria, Canada, Sep. 19-23 1994. IEEE Computer Society Technical Council on Software Engineering.

[Rin96]   D.C. Rine. Structural Defects in Object-Oriented Programming. *Software Engineering Notes*, 21(2):86–88, Mar. 1996.

[RL91]   R.K. Raj and H.M. Levy. On Measuring Abstraction and Reuse in Smalltalk Programs. Unpublished, 1991.

[ROT89]   D.J. Richardson, O. O'Malley, and C. Tittle. Approaches to Specification-Based Testing. Technical Report ICS-TR-89-19, Information and Computer Science, University of California, Irvine, 1989.

[RW85]   S. Rapps and E.J. Weyuker. Selecting Software Test Data Using Data Flow Information. *IEEE Transactions on Software Engineering*, SE-11(4):367–375, Apr. 1985.

[RXR96]   A. Romanovsky, J. Xu, and B. Randell. Exception Handling and Resolution in Distributed Object-Oriented Systems. DeVa (Design for Validation) Esprit Long Term Research Project No. 20072. DeVa TR No. 13, University of Newcastle upon Tyne, 1996.

[RXZ96]   B. Randell, J. Xu, and A.F. Zorzo. Software Fault Tolerance in Object-Oriented Systems. DeVa (Design for Validation) Esprit Long Term Research Project No. 20072. DeVa TR No. 21, University of Newcastle upon Tyne, 1996.

[Rym98]   J. Rymer. Unit and Integration Testing of Objects. In *STAR '98 West*, San Diego, CA, Oct. 1998. Software Quality Engineering.

[Sak89]   M. Sakkinen. Disciplined Inheritance. In *ECOOP '89:Proceedings of the European Conference on Object-Oriented Programming*, 1989.

[SBB87]   R.W. Selby, V.R. Basili, and F.T. Baker. Cleanroom Software Development: An Empirical Evaluation. *IEEE Transactions on Software Engineering*, SE-13(9):1027–1037, Sep. 1987.

[Sch90]   S.R. Schach. *Software Engineering*. Aksen Associates, 1990.

[Sem93]   Semaphore. Glossary of Object-Oriented Terminology, 1993. North Andover, MA.

[Sie94]   S.M. Siegel. OO Integration Testing Specification. In *Seventh International Software Quality Week*, San Francisco, May 1994. Software Research Institute.

[Sie96]   S.M. Siegel. *Object-Oriented Testing: A Hierarchic Approach*. John Wiley & Sons, New York, 1996.

[SM92]   S. Shlaer and S. Mellor. *Object Lifecycles: Modeling the World in States*. Prentice Hall, 1992.

[SM94a]   S. Shlaer and S.J. Mellor. A deeper look at testing and integration, Part 1. *Journal of Object-Oriented Programming*, pages 8–13, Feb. 1994.

[SM94b]   S. Shlaer and S.J. Mellor. A deeper look at testing and integration, Part 2. *Journal of Object-Oriented Programming*, pages 18–22, Jul./Aug. 1994.

[SMT92]   G.M. Schneider, J. Martin, and W.T. Tsai. An experimental study of fault detection in user requirements documents. *ACM Transactions on Software Engineering and Methodology*, 1(2):188–204, Apr. 1992.

[SN94]   E. Siepmann and A.R. Newton. TOBAC: A Test Browser for Testing Object-Oriented Software. In T. Ostrand, editor, *Proceedings of the 1994 International Symposium on Software Testing and Analysis (ISSTA)*, Aug. 17-19 1994.

[Spu94]   David A. Spuler. *C++ and C Debugging, Testing, and Reliability*. Prentice Hall, 1994.

[SR90]   M.D. Smith and D.J. Robson. Object-Oriented Programming - the Problems of Validation. In *Proceedings of the Seventh International Conference on Software Maintenance*, 1990.

[SR92]   M.D. Smith and D.J. Robson. A Framework for Testing Object-Oriented Programs. *Journal of Object-Oriented Programming*, 5(3):45–53, Jun. 1992.

[Str91]   B. Stroustrup. *The C++ Programming Language*. Addison-Wesley, 2nd edition, 1991.

[Str96]   J. Straathof. The Mysteries of Load Testing. *Unix Review*, 14(8):33–40, Jul. 1996.

[TAFM97]   P. Tonella, G. Antoniol, R. Fiutem, and E. Merlo. Flow Insensitive C++ Pointers and Polymorphism Analysis and Its Application to Slicing. In *Proceedings of International Conference on Software Engineering*, pages 433–443, Boston, May 1997. ACM.

[Tay92]   D. Taylor. A Quality-First Program for Object Technology. *Object Magazine*, 2(3):17–18, Jun./Jul. 1992.

[TFW96]   P. Thevenod-Fosse and H. Waeselynck. Towards a Statistical Approach to Testing Object-Oriented Programs. DeVa(Design for Validation) - Esprit Long Term Research Project No. 20072. DeVa TR No. 28, LAAS-CNRS, Toulouse, 1996.

[Thu92]   N.N. Thuy. Testability and Unit Tests in Large Object-Oriented Software. In *Fifth International Software Quality Week*, San Francisco, May 1992. Software Research Institute.

[Thu93]   N.N. Thuy. Design for Quality in Large Object-Oriented Software. In *Sixth International Software Quality Week*, San Francisco, May 1993. Software Research Institute.

[TMTB91]   S. Trausan-Matu, J. Tepandi, and M. Barbuceanu. Validation, verification, and testing of object-oriented programs. In *Ist East European Conference on Object-Oriented Programming*, pages 62–71, Sep. 1991.

[TR92a]   C.D. Turner and D.J. Robson. A Suite of Tools for the State-Based Testing of Object-Oriented Programs. Technical Report TR-14/92, University of Durham, Durham,England, 1992.

[TR92b]   C.D. Turner and D.J. Robson. The Testing of Object-Oriented Programs. Technical Report TR-13/92, University of Durham, England, 1992.

[TR93a]   C.D. Turner and D.J. Robson. Guidance for the Testing of Object-Oriented Programs. Technical Report TR-2/93, University of Durham, England, 1993.

[TR93b]   C.D. Turner and D.J. Robson. State-Based Testing and Inheritance. Technical Report TR-1/93, University of Durham, Durham,England, 1993.

[TR93c]   C.D. Turner and D.J. Robson. The State-Based Testing of Object-Oriented Programs. In *Proceedings of the Nineth International Conference on Software Maintenance*. IEEE Computer Society., 1993.

[TR95]   C.D. Turner and D.J. Robson. A State-base Apporach to the Testing of Class-based Programs. *Software Concepts and Tools*, 16(3):101–112, 1995.

[Tra96]   W. Tracz. Test and Analysis of Software Architectures. In S.J. Zeil, editor, *Proceedings of the 1996 International Symposium on Software Testing and Analysis (ISSTA)*, pages 1–3, San Diego, Jan. 8-10 1996. Association for Computing Machinery. Keynote Address Summary.

[Trida]   Trillium. Model for Telecom Product Development & Support Process Capability. Internet Edition, Dec. 1994. Copyright Bell Canada.

[TZ96]   T.H. Tse and Z. Zu. Test Case Generation for Class-Level Object-Oriented Testing. In *Nineth International Software Quality Week*, San Francisco, May 1996. Software Research Institute.

[VHK97]   J. Vitek, R.N. Horspool, and A. Krall. Efficient Type Inclusion Tests. In *Proceedings of the OOPSLA '97*, pages 142–157. ACM, 1997.

[Voa96]   J.M. Voas. Object-Oriented Software Testability. In S. Bologan and G. Bucci, editors, *Third International Conference on Achieving Quality in Software*, pages 279–290, London, 1996. Chapman and Hall.

[Voa97]   J. Voas. How Assertions Can Increase Test Effectiveness. *IEEE Software*, pages 118–122, Mar./Apr. 1997.

[WA97]   L.J. White and K. Abdullah. A Firewall Approach for the Regression Testing of Object-Oriented Software. In *Tenth Interna-*

tional Software Quality Week, San Francisco, May 1997. Software Research Inc.

[WBWW90] R. Wirfs-Brock, B. Wilkerson, and L. Wiener. *Designing Object-Oriented Software.* Prentice Hall, 1990.

[Wei92] Gerald M. Weinberg. *Quality Software Management: Systems Thinking*, volume 1. Dorset House, 1992.

[Wey86] E.J. Weyuker. Axiomatizing Software Test Data Adequacy. *IEEE Transactions on Software Engineering*, SE-12(12):1128–1138, Dec. 1986.

[Wey88] E.J. Weyuker. The Evaluation of Program-Based Software Test Data Adequacy Criteria. *Communications of the ACM*, 31(6):668–675, Jun. 1988.

[WF84] G.M. Weinberg and D.P. Freedman. Reviews, Walkthroughs, and Inspections. *IEEE Transactions on Software Engineering*, SE-10:68–72, Jan. 1984.

[WH95] P. Walsh and D. Hoffman. Hardware Techniques for Testing Software Components. In *IEEE Pacific Rim Conference on Communications, Computers, and Signal Processing*, pages 128–130. IEEE Computer Society, 1995.

[Win90] T.L. Winfrey. Testing Object-Oriented Programs by Mutually Suspicious Parties. Technical Report CUCS-041-90, Columbia University, New York, 1990.

[WK] C.-M. Wang and Y.S. Kuo. Class Exerciser: A Basic Tool for Object-Oriented Development. In *1995 Asia Pacific Software Engineering Conference*, pages 108–116. IEEE Computer Society.

[WKC+97] Y. Wang, G. King, I. Court, M. Ross, and G. Staples. On Testable Object-Oriented Programming. *Software Engineering Notes*, 22(4):84–90, Jul. 1997.

[Woo96] A. Wood. Predicting Software Reliability. *IEEE Computer*, 29(11):69–77, Nov. 1996.

[WR94] C. Wohlin and P. Runeson. Certification of Software Components. *IEEE Transactions on Software Engineering*, 20(6):494–499, Jun. 1994.

[XRZ96] J. Xu, Randell.B., and A.F. Zorzo. Implementing Software Fault Tolerance in C++ and Open C++: An Object-Oriented and Reflective Approach. DeVa (Design for Validation) Esprit Long Term Research Project No. 20072. DeVa TR No. 01, University of Newcastle upon Tyne, 1996.

[YOO83] S. Yamada, M. Ohba, and S. Osaki. S-Shaped Reliability Growth Modeling for Software Error Detection. *IEEE Transactions on Reliability*, pages 475–484, Dec. 1983.

[YOO86] S. Yamada, H. Ohtera, and K. Okumoto. Software Reliability Growth Models with Testing Effort. *IEEE Transactions on Reliability*, pages 19–23, Apr. 1986.

[YT86] S.S. Yau and J.J.P. Tsai. A Survey of Software Design Techniques. *IEEE Transactions on Software Engineering*, SE-12(6):713–721, Jun. 1986.

[ZCU96] J. Zhao, J. Cheng, and K. Ushijima. Static Slicing of Concurrent Object-Oriented Programs. In *20th International Computer Soft-*

ware and Applications Conference (COMPSAC'96), pages 39–55, 1996.

[ZHK92]   S. Zweben, W. Heym, and J. Kimmich. Systematic Testing of Data Abstractions Based on Software Specifications. *Journal of Software Testing, Verification and Reliability*, 1(4):39–55, 1992.

[ZOPS97]   J. Zhuo, P. Oman, R. Pichai, and S. Sahni. Using Relative Complexity to Allocate Resources in Gray-Box Testing of Object-Oriented Code. In *Fourth International Software Metrics Symposium (METRICS '97)*, Alburquerque, NM, Nov. 1997. IEEE Computer Society Technical Council on Software Engineering.

Index